Boston Marathon – How

Boston Marathon

How to Qualify!

Jeff Galloway

Meyer & Meyer Sport

British Library Cataloguing in Publication Data
A catalogue record for this book is available from the British Library

Jeff Galloway
Boston Marathon – How to Qualify!
Maidenhead: Meyer & Meyer Sport (UK) Ltd., 2010
ISBN 978-1-84126-354-0

© 2010 Meyer & Meyer Sport (UK) Ltd.
2nd Edition 2012
Aachen, Adelaide, Auckland, Budapest, Cape Town, Graz, Indianapolis,
Maidenhead, Olten (CH), Singapore, Toronto
Member of the World
Sport Publishers' Association (WSPA)
www.w-s-p-a.org

Printed and bound by: B.O.S.S Druck und Medien GmbH, Germany
ISBN 978-1-84126-354-0
E-Mail: info@m-m-sports.com
www.m-m-sports.com

Contents

10 What if? Making Adjustments Due to Non-perfect Conditions.............97
- Race weekend doesn't match up with the training plan
- If race day conditions are not right...
- Injury interruption
- Sickness interruption
- Career, vacation, family interruptions
- Cross training can keep you fit, if you must stop running

11 The Galloway Run-Walk-Run Method.......................................101
"Walk breaks give you control over your training and your fatigue."

- Walk before you get tired
- A short and gentle walking stride
- No need to ever eliminate the walk breaks
- How to keep track of the walk breaks
- Strategies by pace per mile

12 The "Magic Mile" is Your Reality Check 105
- The best predictor of performance
- How to do the "MM"
- Galloway's Performance Predictor
- The "leap of faith" goal prediction—how much?

13 Your Journal—The Best Planning and Evaluation Tool 111
- The planning process
- The data recording
- Morning pulse as a guide for overstress

14 Form Improvement Drills—To Make Running Faster and Easier 117

15 The Principles of Great Running Form 121
- I believe that running is an inertial activity
- Relaxed muscles
- The big three: posture, stride and bounce

16 Hill Training Builds Strength—And More...............................127
- The Hill Workout
- Hill Running Form
- Hill training strengthens lower legs and improves running form
- Running faster on hills in races
- Downhill form
- Biggest mistakes: too long a stride, bouncing too much

- Cross training for the upper body
- Weight training
- Don't do these on a non-running day!

- Cramps in the muscles
- Upset stomach or diarrhea
- Headache

1 The Power of Boston: Why is the Boston Marathon the Greatest?

There is no other marathon in the world that has such history and prestige, and has been run every year since the genesis of our sport. There are races with more scenic courses, higher enrollment, and more prize money. But the BAA Marathon in Boston is a legend and continues to be the top draw among serious marathoners around the world.

In 1896, the first marathon race was run from the plain of Marathon to Athens, to close out the first edition of the Modern Olympic Games. The concept of the event was powerful and many cities wanted to replicate this. New York held one race in the Fall of 1896, but did not continue. Boston waited until about one year after the Athens race to hold their first race in 1897. The history of Paul Revere's ride got tangled up in the story somewhere, and the Massachusetts Patriot's Day holiday became the day (3rd Monday in April). But the concept was the same as the original Olympic race: start 25 miles outside the city and finish in the historic city center. Just as many of the governmental guarantees of freedom were debated in the agora of Athens in 490 BC, the origins of the American spirit can be traced to Boston.

There is no better weekend experience for a runner than that leading up to Patriot's Day each year. The feeling of mutual respect is similar to that experienced at the Olympics: each person had to achieve a high standard to enroll in this race and a feeling of excellence permeates the race activities, clinics, restaurants, lineup and the race itself.

Throughout history, many countries have used the Boston Marathon to select their Olympic teams. Until the late 1970's, Boston was the unofficial world championship each year. Today there are several top races with deep world class fields, but none has surpassed the bragging rights of winning the Boston Marathon.

Boston families and groups of friends have established their territories along the race route and pack the race route even in the rain. I've never experienced a more passionate group of spectators.

Most find that the journey to qualify requires sacrifice, fatigue, aches, pains and frustrations. But I've never heard anyone say that it wasn't worth the struggle.

2 My All-Time Favorite Marathon: Sharing Boston 1996 with my Dad

Not because it was the 100th running of Boston... Not because it was my 100th marathon...

Before I started running, I had been a fat and inactive kid. Like many boys, my dad was my hero—I wanted to be an athlete as he had been. I tried football, in which he had achieved "all-state" status. By the end of that season I knew that my temperament wasn't right for the sport that was supposed to "make a man of you."

My dad suggested that I try cross country/distance running, probably because he thought I might burn off some of my extra fat. When I heard from several of the lazy kids that the track coach was lenient and I might pass the time hiding out in the woods near the track, I signed up. But an upper classman invited me to run with his group, and I enjoyed the jokes, discussions and gossip during the run. After 10 weeks, I was hooked on running. Dad was quietly pleased with my interest in running, and supplied me with several training books (including Arthur Lydiard's first book) which opened up a new way of thinking about running in the early ,60s.

As I moved on to college, I became more fit, while Dad became obese—more than 65 pounds heavier than his football weight. As I continued to read and expand the running and fitness library that Dad had provided in my high school years, I became concerned for his health. When I suggested that he simply walk around the park in front of his office, he had one excuse after another. Increasingly his attitude became more negative, he had no energy after work, and his varicose vein pain and allergy problems became worse each year. After several years of discussions, I stopped arguing with him.

The wake up call came at a high school reunion. During the weekend, the former football team assembled, and at age 52 only 12 out of 25 were alive. Each death was due to lifestyle degenerative disease and Dad had recently been told by his doctor that he was headed down the same path. On the long drive back home, something clicked, and he decided to get back in shape the next day.

The next afternoon, Elliott Galloway started around the park in front of his office and could not make it to the first telephone pole. He was out of breath, exhausted and embarrassed. Two days later he was out there again with the mission to reach one more telephone pole. He continued on this trek and within 3 months could make it around the 3 mile loop. After another 90 days he ran two loops which empowered him to run the big hometown event, the Peachtree 10K. Dad didn't stop. Seven years later he was running marathons, had shed 55 pounds and had turned his attitude around. The only time that his varicose veins and allergy aggravation kicked in was when he was unable to run.

Throughout his life, Dad had a heart rhythm issue. At the age of 75, he was running a race every weekend, including a marathon or two every year. While Dr John Cantwell encouraged Dad to run, John was concerned about the significant stress of a marathon, on someone who pushed himself to the limit in every race (Dad never listened to my kinder, gentler advice). He stuck a deal with Dr. Cantwell: his last marathon would be the 1996 Boston Marathon. It would be my 100th marathon, but clearly the one that I will remember most, for the rest of my life.

While we had run the same marathons, on the same days, this would be the first one that we were to run together, the whole way. Each mile was filled with his philosophy, my questions and our good memories. We talked about the fact that only 23 Bostons had been run when Dad was born. I wanted him to take walk breaks every 3 minutes but he didn't want to walk at all. We compromised by walking every mile. He didn't often follow my suggestions.

This was my 5th Boston, but the others had been fiercely competitive efforts. This time we shared views on the scenery, enjoyed and interacted with the energetic crowd, talked about history. Some of the landmarks I had never seen due to my competitive tunnel vision. Dad should have walked every 3 minutes, and slowed down during the last 6 miles, but we savored every minute.

As we made the final turn, and looked down the long straight to the finish banner, Dad took off. We were zooming toward a time barrier which we were determined to break and we did: 5:59:48. As he recounted the race, numerous times, he explained that he would have run a lot faster if I hadn't held him back. I never disagreed.

Now that I've crossed the mid 60s, my Dad is my hero...again.

3 Six Steps to Qualifying for the Boston Marathon

In this book you'll find the resources to train for the goal you will need to qualify for the Boston Marathon. In addition, you'll learn how realistic it is for you to meet your goal, make adjustments, and solve problems along the way. Your resource for the latest logistical information is www.bostonmarathon.com. This book will give information listed as of the writing of the book. Some of the dates and rules may change from year to year—so consult this website for the latest information.

1. Visit www.bostonmarathon.com to find the time you will need to qualify, based upon your age on the day of the next running of the Boston Marathon. For example, if you are 49 years old now, but will turn 50 before the Boston Marathon (April of the next year) you will need to meet the 50-54 standard. Currently, the organization in charge (BAA) allows times run up to 18 months before the race date desired—but check on this. The field is limited to 25,000 runners, and has been closing in late January or early February before the race date. Because this is a "first come, first served" system, get your entry in early.

2. Pick the training schedule in this book that applies to your goal. It helps to have the full term for best results. To learn how all of the elements of training fit together, I conduct running schools in various locations and weekend beach retreats. Be sure to subscribe to my free newsletter for updates:

www.JeffGalloway.com

3. Pick several races that have courses which offer the best chance of qualifying. These races must have "certified" courses. This means that the distance has been determined to be accurate by the governing body of our sport: USA Track and Field. I have included the current top 20+ in this book, according to www.marathonguide.com, which is a great resource in choosing races. Another resource is www.runnersworld.com. Because there are many variables beyond your control that affect your finish time, it's best to have 3 or 4 options, which are 3-4 weeks apart. If you get into one of the races and it's not your day, you can run at training run pace, and save your race effort for the next one on the schedule.

4. Use the "magic mile," explained in this book, to monitor progress. It is productive for most to run marathons as training runs before you are physically ready to qualify, to gain marathon racing experience. Fine-tune your training to improve your times, as noted in this book.

5. Once you have your time, register online at www.bostonmarathon.com, secure a hotel room ASAP and arrange for your transportation. Congratulations!

6. If this is your first Boston, I strongly suggest that you not try to run all-out. If you slow down by about a minute per mile from what you could run, you can enjoy the weekend, the crowds, your fellow runners and the wonderful Boston restaurants/taverns afterwards.

4 How to Choose the Right Course— Some are Faster

All courses are not created equal. By doing a little research and choosing the right venue, you can improve your chance of qualifying. In the process you'll probably discover a number of other races you want to put on your marathon "to do" list.

There are several websites that allow you compare courses—especially **www. marathonguide.com** and **www.runnersworld.com**. Look through these for significant elevation changes, typical temperature, quantity of turns, and any other factors that either tend to help you or hurt you.

Pick 3 candidates that are 3-4 weeks apart each. In my experience, you have about a 25 % chance of having somewhat perfect conditions on any given day of the year. By picking 3 that are 3-4 weeks apart, you will be able to run the first one or two as a training run, when facing challenges such as temperature increase, infection, minor injury, etc. This means that you don't have to waste 6 months of training if things aren't perfect on the big day. It helps to add 3 additional miles to marathon distance to gain maximum benefit from the 29 mile distance—as the endurance effect will only last for 4 weeks.

Read the runner reviews of races. These are usually quite honest, giving you a good feeling for the race, while usually presenting the problems that tend to occur.

When there are more than 10,000 runners, you will tend to run significantly farther than race distance. Many of my e-coach clients who run in races with more than 30,000 runners often find that they register more than a mile farther on their GPS devices. For the best chance in achieving time goals, it's best to run in races with 5000 or less, on roads that are not too narrow or have too many turns.

Those who train mostly in rolling terrain may not run as fast on a perfectly flat course, because they will fatigue the flat muscles quickly. Those who don't train on hills should avoid hilly marathon courses.

Some race routes have significant downhill sections. For those who have trained for this, there is often a significant time improvement. Without downhill training, however, the downhill in the race can be abusive, and result in a slowdown at the end, with extended recovery.

There's no way you can predict the temperature. The research shows that you'll run faster when the temperature is below 60F (14C) than when it's hotter. By looking at the average high temperature, you can find a place where it is more likely to be cool. But as you know with the weather, there are no guarantees.

According to **www.marathonguide.com**, the courses that produced the highest percentage of Boston qualifiers (2008) are the following (for current information check that website or the site of the marathon itself):

Bay State Marathon, MA—38 % (Oct)

Mohawk-Hudson River Marathon, NY—32 % (Oct)

Road 2 Hope/Hamilton Marathon, Canada—31 % (Nov)

Newport Marathon, OR—28.8 % (May)

California Intl Marathon, CA—28.2 % (Dec)

Steamtown Marathon, PA—28 % (Oct)

Wineglass Marathon, NY—27.8 % (Oct)

Tucson Marathon, AZ—27.2 % (Dec)

Grand Rapids Marathon, MI—25.3 (Oct)

Royal Victoria Marathon, Canada—24.9 % (Oct)

Snickers Marathon, GA—24.3 % (Mar)

Rocket City Marathon, AL—22.9 (Dec)

Hyannis Marathon, MA—22.3 % (Feb)

Columbus Marathon, OH—22.1 % (Oct)

Coeur d'Alene Marathon, ID—21.6 % (May)

Louisville Marathon, KY—21.6 % (Oct)

Regina Marathon, Canada—21.4 % (Sep)

Pocono Mountain Marathon, PA—21.3 (May)

North Central Trail Marathon, MD—20.8 (Nov)

St George Marathon, UT—20.7 % (Oct)

Towpath Marathon, OH—20.7 % (Oct)

5   A Tour of the Boston Course with Bill Rodgers

Secrets of the Boston Course as Told by Bill Rodgers

Bill Rodgers, Amby Burfoot and I ran together at Wesleyan University (Middletown, CT) during the 60's. None of us showed much national running potential as high school athletes and were by-passed in the offering of scholarships. Wesleyan didn't even offer athletic scholarships. Early in his collegiate career, Amby envisioned that his best event was not on the collegiate competition schedule. While competing for the team, Amby added miles to his training, traveled to various New England road races, and surprised us and the world by winning the Boston Marathon during the Spring of his senior year. This set a standard of excellence which energized Bill and myself. Four years later I made the ,72 Olympic team. Bill waited a bit longer but surpassed our accomplishments by winning the Boston Marathon in ,75, ,78, ,79 and ,80, breaking the course record twice.

When I decided to write this book, I couldn't think of anyone who knew the Boston course better than Bill. For years he trained on the course, did repeats on Heartbreak Hill. So on the appointed day, just after 12 noon we arrived at the starting line, ate a Greek style pizza at "Bills Pizza" near the start (no affiliation with Bill Rodgers) and began our tour. Bill's statements are in quotes.

Mile 1

The elevation at the starting line is 490 feet. Randomly, the year that Phidippides (or whomever) ran from the battle of Marathon to Athens was 490 BC. The staging ground, leading to the start is flat. But just after crossing the line you'll get a downhill boost for about seven tenths of a mile. "Don't go too fast here—it's very steep in places. It's really crowded—don't trip."

Mile 2

There are slight ups and mostly gentle downs as the course (on Route 135) moves through the hamlet of Ashland, the original starting location of the Boston Marathon. The first race in 1897 was started by the first Olympic champion in the 400 meters and 100 meters, Thomas Burke, who called the 15 man field to the line he had drawn on the dirt road, and said "Go." According to reports, there were 10 finishers. In 1924 the Boston Marathon officials pushed the start back to Hopkington.

"Many runners lose it, because they don't slow down when the course levels out—and pay for this later. I was able to use the hills later in the course because I saved myself during the first half of the race. I never worried about the finish time—just tried to do my best."

Mile 3

Moving out of Ashland, the course is relatively flat, but still gently downhill. "Ashland is where I received my first "professional" payment. I was paid $50 to talk to the Ashland cross country team."

Mile 4

Mostly a flat mile with minor rolling. The Wildwood Cemetery is on the right near the 4 mile mark.

"I disagree with the decision not to allow a World Record on the Boston course. The IAAF (which sanctions records) says there is too much of an elevation drop from Hopkington to downtown Boston. But only one world's best time has ever been run here by the men."

Mile 5

The elevation changes continue to be minimal. There's a reservoir on the left for the full length of this mile. Just before the 5-mile mark, there's a slight uphill, followed by a slight downhill for 200 yards. Bill says "You will have energy at this point, and may be tempted to pick up the pace. But it is still crowded—settle in and save your energy."

Mile 6

Approaching Framingham, the course is mostly flat with minor ups and downs. In the early days of the Boston race, this was where runners received their first time check (one fourth of the way to the finish). There were no mile marks nor pace times given back then. "This is classic small town America, town square, residents sitting in lawn chairs—usually a big turnout, here. The crowds start to build here—it gets more and more exciting as the race continues."

"There is a large Brazilian community here. One year I couldn't get to the start to help with festivities because the Brazilians were celebrating their team's victory in the World Cup."

Mile 7

Course elevation shows a slight downhill—most don't notice this. About 6.3 miles you'll see Farm Pond on your left. Just after mile 7 you'll pass Mary Dennison Playground on your right.

Mile 8

The course flattens after Framingham, with a slight uphill of about 200 yards in the middle of this mile. Lined with repair shops, hardware supplies, etc., this is not the most scenic part of the course. There aren't a lot of spectators along this line of businesses because it's a holiday and the road is closed.

Mile 9

After the 8 mile mark there is a gentle downhill, but most don't notice it. As you approach the 9-mile marker, notice Fisk Reservoir on the right. "I believe this is where Boston champion Tarzan Brown jumped in the lake, and came back to win the race in the early days."

Mile 10

There is a slight uphill that is quite gentle, leading into the pleasant town of Natick. "Natick has a beautiful town square and big crowds."

Miles 11 and 12

For most of the first mile, the course seems to be flat with a very slight uphill. Just after the 11-mile mark, the elevation drops for about a mile with only a few slight upgrades. "At this point you begin to hear the cheering of the Wellesley College students, about a mile ahead. The screaming excitement pulls you along."

Mile 13

After mile mark # 12, with Morse Pond on your left, there is a very gentle uphill with some slight rolling down. Your eardrums will get a workout from the Wellesley students. Moving into the upscale town of Wellesley, there are huge crowds, parks, and interesting houses. As you leave the town, you'll pass the halfway point. "During the Boston Spring you never know about the weather: sometimes you see beautiful blooms and sometimes you have the last chill of winter."

Miles 14 and 15

There is a light uphill trend to these two miles, with a few short and gentle downs. Just after the 15-mile mark, be prepared for a significant downhill of about half a mile. "I made my move here. When I lived near the course, I trained on this stretch often and practiced this. This was a huge advantage for me."

Miles 16 and 17

After the 16-mile mark, there's a significant uphill over I-95, which continues past the 17-mile mark. This is the first of 4 hills in a row, with Heartbreak Hill as the finale. The first upgrade is gradual but can take it out of you if you push a little too hard.

Miles 18 and 19

After the 17-mile mark, the course makes a right turn onto Commonwealth Avenue. The grass median of this divided street is crammed with spectators whose mission is to cheer you up the hill and onto the finish. Many runners get a bit too excited at this point and spend resources that are better saved for later. A few hundred yards up Commonwealth, the first hill ends, followed by some flat and a slight downhill. At about 17.5 miles you'll ascend the second hill, which is only about 250-300 yards. "There's a really extended downhill (of about seven tenths of a mile] after this hill which I used to recover."

Mile 20

At about 19.5 miles, just before starting up the third hill, Bill told us to look to the left. Slightly hidden in the trees is a bronze statue of two runners. We stopped and paid our tribute to the saint of the Boston Marathon, Johnny Kelley. Johnny is sculpted as a young man and then as the legend who ran the race until he was 84, his 58th finish. He won the race twice. He finished 18th in the 1936 Olympics, in Berlin, where he met the first Olympic marathon champion (1896) Spiridon Louis. Runner's World magazine recognized Kelley as "The Runner of the Century."

After the 3rd hill, about 300 yards long, the elevation is fairly flat for about half a mile, passing the 20-mile mark. Then you see it—Heartbreak Hill. "Heartbreak is 600 meters long, not a steep grade, but tough at this stage of the course. I used to do hill repeats on Heartbreak—6 of them."

Miles 21 and 22

At the top of the hill, there's a fairly flat stretch for about a third of a mile passing the 21st mile mark, and then you'll head downhill for about a mile and a half. You'll pass Evergreen Cemetery (where many good runners have dropped out) then Chestnut Hill Reservoir. Just before Cleveland Circle (at 21.5 miles), look to the left. As we drove by, Bill pointed to a "cut and nails" shop which was an important landmark: the location of the first Bill Rodgers Running Center (now located in Faneuil Hall, in the historic district of Boston).

As you turn left onto Beacon Street, there is a slight uphill for several hundred yards—most of it very gradual. "On Beacon Street, you feel you're in ,real Boston.' This pulls you to the finish line." Bill likes the fact that you only see about 300 yards ahead, at any point. "From here to the finish, the crowds are great." Right around the 23-mile mark, you will start another gradual downhill for about a mile.

Miles 23 and 24

As you run through the neighborhoods along Beacon Street, there will be glimpses of the Boston skyline. Around mile 24 the course becomes flat and you may see the Citgo sign, which is still a mile away. "Each landmark tells you that you're getting closer."

Mile 25

As you go by the Citgo sign, you have about a mile to go. Crossing over I-90, you'll see the Prudential Center in the distance which is very close to the finish. At about 25.8 you'll pass the Eliot Lounge turning right onto Hereford St, quickly passing 26 miles and then turning left onto Boylston Street. The finish structure welcomes you home, pulling you to Copley Square. The crowds are amazing.

"I hope to see you there—I'll be cheering for you!"
Bill Rodgers

Four-Time Boston Marathon Champion

6   How to Qualify and Enter

2013 BOSTON MARATHON QUALIFYING TIMES
(Subject to change – check www.BAA.org site for current information)

AGE GROUP	MEN	WOMEN
18-34	3hrs 05min	3hrs 35min
35-39	3hrs 10min	3hrs 40min
40-44	3hrs 15min	3hrs 45min
45-49	3hrs 25min	3hrs 55min
50-54	3hrs 30min	4hrs 00min
55-59	3hrs 40min	4hrs 10min
60-64	3hrs 55min	4hrs 25min
65-69	4hrs 10min	4hrs 40min
70-74	4hrs 25min	4hrs 55min
75-79	4hrs 40min	5hrs 10min
80 and over	4hrs 55min	5hrs 25min

Unlike previous years, an additional 59 seconds will NOT be accepted for each age group time standard.

Because a significant increase in the number of qualifiers the organizing committee of the BAA has revised their qualifying standards and the procedure for entering. To receive the latest news on qualifying and entering, carefully read the information at www.BAA.org website.

1. Choose the qualifying race or races which have been certified and measured according to standards accepted by the BAA. When in doubt you can ask the race officials of a prospective race for the certification number of their course. Most of the recognized marathons in the US have met this standard – but you should check.

2. Carefully read the "qualifying" and "registration process" sections on the BAA. org website, and follow their directions. It is suggested that you have an internet connection available at the date/time listed, and register as quickly as you can.

3. Example: Starting with the 2012 race, a "rolling admission" schedule was used. Those who achieved qualifying times that are 20 minutes or more faster than the standard for their age/gender were allowed to enter during the first two days, and then those finished 10 minutes faster than their standard could enter during a two day period. If space was still available, those who ran 5 minutes faster were given three days to enter and then all qualifiers could try to enter.

4. During the first week of registration, applicants were notified as their qualifying performance verified, as all qualifying times are subject to review and verification.

7 A Blending of Key Elements

Training for top performance often brings out the best in an athlete. But to be at your best for your goal race it's not enough that all of the training elements have to come together. During the tough workouts and the race itself, each runner must face doubts, often feeling unequal to the task. Mental training can improve motivation as it allows for continued pushing even when under duress. But during the real tough days there will be times when each athlete must dig a little deeper while monitoring the early warning signs of injury.

A proven strategy to Boston

A high percentage of my coaching clients who have followed the program below have set personal records (PRs) or qualified for Boston. Each component is an important member of the "team" of elements that can lead to a performance peak. When all of these are blended correctly, improvements and adaptations are integrated into the internal workings of your muscle cells, cardiovascular system, orthopedic structures and muscle function to produce a synergy of performance.

Balance is crucial. You may perform the best workouts in your life, but if you don't have enough rest between workouts, the body will not rebound, and residual fatigue or damage will reduce the final result. When workouts are too far ahead of current ability, the muscles may suffer from lingering fatigue at the start of the marathon, with a slowdown at the end.

1. Set realistic goals each season. Use the current performance or the "magic mile" explained in this book to set up a "leap of faith" goal. See page 107.

2. The body responds better to gradual improvement allowing the many internal systems to improve your infrastructure without being exhausted and/or breaking down. A 3 % performance improvement is realistic during a training season, while a 5 % improvement is possible but very challenging. See pages 107-108.

3. So it's better to project a modest improvement of 3 % which is more likely to lead to steady and progressive changes over several years.

4. Use the "magic mile" time trial in this book to monitor improvement—a reality check. See page 105.

5. The long runs are the most important training component in a marathon training program. They will bestow the endurance necessary for your goal. You cannot go too slow on the long ones. I recommend running at least 2 minutes per mile lower than your "magic mile" is predicting in the marathon itself—but it is better to go at a pace that is 3-4 min/mi slower. Be sure to read the "Galloway Run-Walk-Run Method" chapter in this book. Long ones must be done slowly with liberal walk breaks for fast recovery. For maximum benefit, build the series of long ones up to 29 miles, as noted in the following schedules. By going longer than marathon distance you may never "hit the wall" again.

6. On non-long-run weekends, run a series of one mile (or 2 mile) repeat workouts. These train you to deal with the physical and psychological challenges during the last 6 miles of your race where your time goal is either made, or compromised. These push back your performance wall—both mentally and physically. See # 11 on instructions with schedule.

7. Insert sufficient rest between the stress workouts to allow all the body parts to rebuild—rest is crucial if you want to benefit from the hard workouts instead of increasing the fatigue level or breaking down with injury. On low mileage days, even if you have a form drill or hill workout scheduled, if you feel that you need to jog easily on that day, and shorten the mileage, do so.

8. Back off when your "gut instinct" tells you that you may be getting injured. The prime reason that runners don't achieve their goal is "injury interruption" with the loss of capacity. When your intuition tells you that it may be injury, stop the workout and take an extra day or two off.

9. The cadence drills help you become a more efficient runner. These are scheduled into the short runs during the week. See page 107.

10. The acceleration-gliders train the muscles to "shift gears" when needed, so that you're ready for any challenge. They also help you glide to save muscle resources while maintaining speed. See pages 118-119.

11. Hills build just the right amount of strength to deal with hills on your race course. They also help you run more efficiently. See the Hill section pp 127-129.

8 For Extra Credit

Additional training elements that may give you 1-2 minutes each

A second workout

On the short mileage days (particularly Tuesday and Friday) you can add a 3-5 mile easy run. This is usually done early in the morning, which tends to help the legs feel better for the afternoon workout. Some runners, however, tend to run their scheduled run in the morning and will jog very easily in the afternoon.

Compression sleeves for the calves

I use the Zenzah calf sleeve for my calf muscles on long runs and races—my legs feel better during and afterward. Research shows that sleeves can improve performance, enhance blood flow in the crucial calf muscle, and promote quicker recovery. Those who have a family history of blood clots should know that calf compression sleeves have helped those with this condition.

Water running

This is the only cross training mode that I believe can improve running performance. When done correctly, once a week for at least 15 minutes, running form tends to improve. When done on several days per week, there seems to be a performance benefit. This exercise is explained in the cross training section of this book.

Mental Training—to keep going when it's tough

Read the "Mental Toughness" chapter in this book and design your mental training workouts that can help you push on, when you don't feel like you can. As you discover where you tend to have mental letdowns, you can structure your mental training to compensate. To improve the effectiveness of the mental training, practice the techniques during your speed workouts, or race rehearsal segments.

Bio Feedback from Heart Monitoring

The heart monitor is not necessary for achieving your goal. But if you have this technology: During some of your race rehearsal segments or speed sessions, for example, try to keep your heart rate below 80 % by fine-tuning your running form. This not only conserves resources, but also teaches you to run more efficiently.

9 Training Schedules

Following are day-by-day training programs for either your goal race, or for running faster in the Boston Marathon. They contain the minimum that I've found necessary to prepare for each goal listed. If you are already running more than is listed on the schedule, it's usually OK to continue to do so. The key workouts are done on the weekend, and involve increases in mileage and speed (mile or two mile repetitions). Those who also increase the mileage and intensity of the "maintenance runs" during the week have experienced a high risk of injury, lingering fatigue and slower times at the end of the program. Remember that stress needs to be balanced with rest.

Note: When running your first Boston Marathon, I recommend that you focus on enjoying the event. Run at least 60 seconds slower per mile after the first mile. This conservative pacing will allow you to enjoy the wonderful crowd, the landmarks, fellow runners and the whole experience. It will take the pressure off during the weekend, allowing you to walk around the historic district, explore the expo, and savor some of the great restaurants.

Time goal 3:05

Note: This is the minimum that I've found necessary to prepare for the goal. If you are already running more than this amount, and are able to recover between workouts, you may continue to do what you are doing – but be careful.

1. To begin this program, you should have run a long run within the past 2 weeks of at least 6 miles. If your long run is not this long, then gradually increase the weekend run to this distance before starting the program.

2. If your current long run is longer than 7 miles, it is possible to start on the week with a long run that is at or slightly longer than the distance of the longest run you have run in the past 2 weeks. For example, if you ran 13 miles, two weeks ago, you could start with week # 8, # 9 or # 10. In this case, you will lose the benefits from the hill workouts, on the short mileage weekends.

3. What is your current level of performance? The "magic mile" time trials, noted by MM on the schedule, will tell you. Read the chapter in this book on "Choosing The Right Goal". Take your current (MM) and multiply by 1.3. This predicts your best possible per mile performance in the marathon under ideal conditions when you've done all of the training. Follow the instructions in that chapter to set a realistic goal and to monitor your progress. The MM is run once, on each weekend noted in the schedule. You can run any pace you wish for the remaining miles assigned on these workouts. To predict that you are ready for a 3:05 goal, you should be able to run a MM time of 5:22 or faster by the end of the training program.

4. What pace should I run on the long runs? Take your current performance level (MM x 1.3) and add 2 minutes. The result is your suggested long run pace per mile on long runs at 60F or cooler. For those who are currently predicting a 3:05 in the marathon, the long run pace should be no faster than 9:10 per mile at 60F and 10:15 at 70F. It is always better to run slower to ensure faster recovery.

5. On long runs, and in the marathon itself, slow down even more when the temperature rises: by 30 seconds a mile for every 5 degrees above 60F.

6. Run-walk-run ratio should correspond to the pace used (See the Run-Walk-Run chapter in this book).

7. Most runners don't improve more than 30 seconds per mile during a 30 week marathon training program. If your goal is more aggressive, you may increase injury stress during the training or may be frustrated with your final time. Use the MM's as reality checks on your current performance level, and remember that they are based upon "ideal projections".

8. Speed repetitions of 2 miles each are listed on the schedule for this goal (8 laps around a 400 meter track). During each 2 miler, run the first and the last 800 meter in 3:20, and run the mile in the middle in 6:30-6:35. At the one mile mark, walk for 15-20 seconds. Stay smooth. If you are struggling to maintain pace, slow

down to run efficiently. If you are slowing down significantly during the second mile, shift to running twice as many one mile repeats. Be sure to read the section in this book on speed training.

9. Warm up for each 2 mile repeat workout by walking for 2-5 minutes, then jog very slowly for 5-10 minutes. Next, do 4-8 acceleration-gliders (see the segment about this in this book). Reverse this process as your warm down, leaving out the acceleration gliders.

10. Recover between each 2 mile repeat by walking and jogging for 5-6 minutes between each. You may choose the amount of walking vs jogging. If you are using a heart monitor, your heart rate should drop below 65% of max heart rate before starting another 2 mile repeat.

11. If you have recovered from the weekend run, during your Tuesday workout, run 2-4 miles at race pace (noted as "p" on the Tue line). After an easy warm-up, run 4 of the acceleration-gliders (Acg). (These are described in the drill section of this book). Then run a mile segment at 7:08, take a 40 sec walk break, and run a second mile with a total time of 14:16, take another 40 sec walk break and continue for 1-2 more miles. This means that you will have to pick up the pace by a few seconds per minute to maintain your 7:08 pace by the watch. Stay smooth. This trains you to run at race pace, taking walk breaks.

12. It is fine to do cross training on Monday and Friday, if you wish. Except for running in the water, cross training doesn't tend to improve performance. Avoid exercises like stair machines (during rest days from running) that use the calf muscles.

13. Be sure to take a vacation from strenuous exercise, the day before your long runs and mile repetitions.

14. On Friday, run a few hill repeats (h), as described in the hill section in this book. The Acg's will get the legs warmed up for the hill accelerations. The length of the hills should be 250 meters to 400 meters. Walk down most of each hill for almost complete recovery.

15. Hills (h) are suggested on short mileage weekends, during the early weeks of the program. Start with 2 hill repeats and increase by one hill on each successive workout until you reach 5 hills, as noted on the schedule. Because Boston has some significant hills in strategic locations, these workouts are helpful. The hills are embedded into the total mileage for the day.

16. Double workouts can be run on Tuesday and Friday. See the chapter in this book called "For Extra Credit".

17. During the last two weeks of the program, you cannot improve performance so avoid running too fast. On some of the short mile days, however, it is OK to run a 2 mile segment running 7:08 pace, while taking a 35 second walk break at the mile mark. This fine-tunes your pace judgement and your mental focus.

18. Never run through pain—read the chapter on injuries if you sense that you have the beginning of an injury.

Mon	Tue (CDAcg/p)	Wed	Thurs (CD)	Fri (Acg/h)	Sat	Sun
Week 1						
off	45 min run	off or XT	30 min run	60 min	off	7 miles
Week 2						
off	45 min run	off/XT	30 min run	60 min	off	8 miles
Week 3						
off	50 min run	off/XT	30 min run	60 min	off	5 mi with 2 hills
Week 4						
off	50 min run	off/XT	30 min run	60 min	off	9.5 miles
Week 5						
off	40 min run	off/XT	30 min run	60 min	off	5 mi with 3 hills
Week 6						
off	50 min run	off/XT	30 min run	60 min	off	11 miles
Week 7						
off	40 min run	off/XT	30 min run	60 min	off	6 mi with 4 hills
Week 8						
off	55 min run	off/XT	30 min run	60 min	off	13 miles
Week 9						
off	40 min run	off/XT	30 min run	60 min	off	6 mi with 5 hills
Week 10						
off	55 min run	off/XT	30 min run	60 min	off	15 miles
Week 11						
off	40 min run	off/XT	30 min run	60 min	off	2 x 2 mile
Week 12						
off	60 min run	off/XT	30 min run	60 min	off	17 miles
Week 13						
off	40 min run	off/XT	30 min run	70 min	off	3 x 2 mile
Week 14						
off	60 min run	off/XT	30 min run	70 min	off	8 miles MM
Week 15						
off	65 min run	off/XT	30 min run	70 min	off	20 miles

Week 16

off	45 min run	off/XT	30 min run	70 min	off	4 x 2 mile

Week 17

off	65 min run	off/XT	30 min run	70 min	off	7 miles MM

Week 18

off	65 min run	off/XT	30 min run	70 min	off	23 miles

Week 19

off	45 min run	off/XT	30 min run	70 min	off	5 x 2 mile

Week 20

off	70 min run	off/XT	30 min run	70 min	off	7 miles MM

Week 21

off	70 min run	off/XT	30 min run	60 min	off	26 miles

Week 22

off	45 min run	off/XT	30 min run	75 min	off	6 miles

Week 23

off	70 min run	off/XT	30 min run	70 min	off	6 x 2 mile

Week 24

off	70 min run	off/XT	30 min run	75 min	off	7 miles MM

Week 25

off	70 min run	off/XT	30 min run	60 min	off	29 miles

Week 26

off	70 min run	off/XT	30 min run	75 min	off	6 miles

Week 27

off	70 min run	off/XT	30 min run	60 min	off	7 x 2 miles

Week 28

off	45 min run	off/XT	30 min run	70 min	off	7 miles

Week 29

off	40 min run	off/XT	30 min run	30 min	off	Goal Race/Boston

Week 30 (Recovery week)

off/XT	30 min run	off/XT	30 min run	off	5 miles	off

Time goal 3:10

Note: This is the minimum that I've found necessary to prepare for the goal. If you are already running more than this amount, and are able to recover between workouts, you may continue to do what you are doing—but be careful.

1. To begin this program, you should have run a long run within the past 2 weeks of at least 6 miles. If your long run is not this long, then gradually increase the weekend run to this distance before starting the program.

2. If your current long run is longer than 7 miles, it is possible to start on the week with a long run that is at or slightly longer than the distance of the longest run you have run in the past 2 weeks. For example, if you ran 13 miles two weeks ago, you could start with week # 8, # 9 or # 10. In this case, you will lose the benefits from the hill workouts on the short mileage weekends.

3. What is your current level of performance? The "magic mile" time trials, noted by MM on the schedule, will tell you. Read the chapter in this book on "Choosing the Right Goal..." Take your current MM and multiply by 1.3. This predicts your best possible per mile performance in the marathon under ideal conditions when you've done all of the training. Follow the instructions in that chapter to set a realistic goal and to monitor your progress. The MM is run once on each weekend noted in the schedule. You can run any pace you wish for the remaining miles assigned on these workouts. To predict that you are ready for a 3:10 goal, you should be able to run a MM time of 5:30 or faster by the end of the training program.

4. What pace should I run on the long runs? Take your current performance level (MM x 1.3) and add 2 minutes. The result is your suggested long run pace per mile on long runs at 60F or cooler. For those who are currently predicting a 3:10 in the marathon, the long run pace should be no faster than 9:15 per mile at 60F and 10:15 at 70F. It is always better to run slower to ensure faster recovery.

5. On long runs, and in the marathon itself, slow down even more when the temperature rises: by 30 seconds a mile for every 5 degrees above 60F.

6. Run-Walk-Run ratio should correspond to the pace used (See the Run-Walk-Run chapter in this book).

7. Most runners don't improve more than 30 seconds per mile during a 30-week marathon training program. If your goal is more aggressive, you may increase injury stress during the training or may be frustrated with your final time. Use the MMs as reality checks on your current performance level, and remember that they are based upon "ideal projections."

8. Speed repetitions of 2 miles each are listed on the schedule for this goal (8 laps around a 400 meter track). During each 2 miler, run the first and the last 800 meters in 3:25, and run the mile in the middle in 6:40-6:45. At the one mile mark, walk for 20 seconds. Stay smooth. If you are struggling to maintain pace, slow down to run efficiently. If you are slowing down significantly during the

second mile, shift to running twice as many one mile repeats. Be sure to read the section in this book on speed training.

9. Warm up for each 2 mile repeat workout by walking for 2-5 minutes, then jog very slowly for 5-10 minutes. Next, do 4-8 acceleration-gliders (see the segment about this in this book). Reverse this process as you warm down, leaving out the acceleration gliders.

10. Recover between each 2 mile repeat by walking and jogging for 5-6 minutes between each. You may choose the amount of walking vs. jogging. If you are using a heart monitor, your heart rate should drop below 65 % of max heart rate before starting another 2 mile repeat.

11. If you have recovered from the weekend run, during your Tuesday workout, run 2-4 miles at race pace (noted as "p" on the Tue line). After an easy warm-up, run 4 of the acceleration-gliders (Acg). (These are described in the drill section of this book). Then run a mile segment at 7:15, take a 40 sec walk break, and run a second mile with a total time of 14:30, take another 40 sec walk break and continue for 1-2 more miles. This means that you will have to pick up the pace by a few seconds per minute to maintain your 7:15 pace by the watch. Stay smooth. This trains you to run at race pace, taking walk breaks.

12. It is fine to do cross training on Monday and Friday, if you wish. Except for running in the water, cross training doesn't tend to improve performance. Avoid exercises like stair machines (during rest days from running) that use the calf muscles.

13. Be sure to take a vacation from strenuous exercise the day before your long runs and mile repetitions.

14. On Friday, run a few hill repeats (h), as described in the hill section in this book. The Acg's will get the legs warmed up for the hill accelerations. The length of the hills should be 250 meters to 400 meters. Walk down most of each hill for almost complete recovery.

15. Hills (h) are suggested on short mileage weekends, during the early weeks of the program. Start with 2 hill repeats and increase by one hill on each successive workout until you reach 5 hills, as noted on the schedule. Because Boston has some significant hills in strategic locations, these workouts are helpful. The hills are embedded into the total mileage for the day.

16. Double workouts can be run on Tuesday and Friday. See the chapter in this book called "For Extra Credit."

17. During the last two weeks of the program, you cannot improve performance so avoid running too fast. On some of the short mile days, however, it is OK to run a 2 mile segment running 7:15 pace, while taking a 40 second walk break at the mile mark. This fine-tunes your pace judgment and your mental focus.

18. Never run through pain—read the chapter on injuries if you sense that you have the beginning of an injury.

Mon	Tue (CDAcg/p)	Wed	Thurs (CD)	Fri (Acg/h)	Sat	Sun
Week 1						
off	45 min run	off or XT	30 min run	60 min	off	7 miles
Week 2						
off	45 min run	off/XT	30 min run	60 min	off	8 miles
Week 3						
off	50 min run	off/XT	30 min run	60 min	off	5 mi with 2 hills
Week 4						
off	50 min run	off/XT	30 min run	60 min	off	9.5 miles
Week 5						
off	40 min run	off/XT	30 min run	60 min	off	5 mi with 3 hills
Week 6						
off	50 min run	off/XT	30 min run	60 min	off	11 miles
Week 7						
off	40 min run	off/XT	30 min run	60 min	off	6 mi with 4 hills
Week 8						
off	55 min run	off/XT	30 min run	60 min	off	13 miles
Week 9						
off	40 min run	off/XT	30 min run	60 min	off	6 mi with 5 hills
Week 10						
off	55 min run	off/XT	30 min run	60 min	off	15 miles
Week 11						
off	40 min run	off/XT	30 min run	60 min	off	2 x 2 mile
Week 12						
off	60 min run	off/XT	30 min run	60 min	off	17 miles
Week 13						
off	40 min run	off/XT	30 min run	70 min	off	3 x 2 mile
Week 14						
off	60 min run	off/XT	30 min run	70 min	off	8 miles MM
Week 15						
off	65 min run	off/XT	30 min run	70 min	off	20 miles

Week 16						
off	45 min run	off/XT	30 min run	70 min	off	4 x 2 mile
Week 17						
off	65 min run	off/XT	30 min run	70 min	off	7 miles MM
Week 18						
off	65 min run	off/XT	30 min run	70 min	off	23 miles
Week 19						
off	45 min run	off/XT	30 min run	70 min	off	5 x 2 mile
Week 20						
off	70 min run	off/XT	30 min run	70 min	off	7 miles MM
Week 21						
off	70 min run	off/XT	30 min run	60 min	off	26 miles
Week 22						
off	45 min run	off/XT	30 min run	75 min	off	6 miles
Week 23						
off	70 min run	off/XT	30 min run	70 min	off	6 x 2 mile
Week 24						
off	70 min run	off/XT	30 min run	75 min	off	7 miles MM
Week 25						
off	70 min run	off/XT	30 min run	60 min	off	29 miles
Week 26						
off	70 min run	off/XT	30 min run	75 min	off	6 miles
Week 27						
off	70 min run	off/XT	30 min run	60 min	off	7 x 2 miles
Week 28						
off	45 min run	off/XT	30 min run	70 min	off	7 miles
Week 29						
off	40 min run	off/XT	30 min run	30 min	off	Goal Race/Boston
Week 30 (Recovery week)						
off/XT	30 min run	off/XT	30 min run	off	5 miles	off

Time goal 3:15

Note: This is the minimum that I've found necessary to prepare for the goal. If you are already running more than this amount, and are able to recover between workouts, you may continue to do what you are doing—but be careful.

1. To begin this program, you should have run a long run within the past 2 weeks of at least 6 miles. If your long run is not this long, then gradually increase the weekend run to this distance before starting the program.

2. If your current long run is longer than 7 miles, it is possible to start on the week with a long run that is at or slightly longer than the distance of the longest run you have run in the past 2 weeks. For example, if you ran 13 miles two weeks ago, you could start with week # 8, # 9 or # 10. In this case, you will lose the benefits from the hill workouts on the short mileage weekends.

3. What is your current level of performance? The "magic mile" time trials, noted by MM on the schedule, will tell you. Read the chapter in this book on "Choosing the Right Goal..." Take your current MM and multiply by 1.3. This predicts your best possible per mile performance in the marathon under ideal conditions when you've done all of the training. Follow the instructions in that chapter to set a realistic goal and to monitor your progress. The MM is run once on each weekend noted in the schedule. You can run any pace you wish for the remaining miles assigned on these workouts. To predict a 3:15 marathon performance, your MM should be 5:35 or faster by the end of the program.

4. What pace should I run on the long runs? Take your current performance level (MM x 1.3) and add 2 minutes. The result is your suggested long run pace per mile on long runs at 60F or cooler. For those who are currently predicting a 3:15 in the marathon, the long run pace should be no faster than 9:30 per mile at 60F and 10:30/mi at 70F. It is always better to run slower to ensure faster recovery.

5. On long runs, and in the marathon itself, slow down even more when the temperature rises: by 30 seconds a mile for every 5 degrees above 60F.

6. Run-Walk-Run ratio should correspond to the pace used (See the Run-Walk-Run chapter in this book).

7. Most runners don't improve more than 30 seconds per mile during a 30-week marathon training program. If your goal is more aggressive, you may increase injury stress during the training or may be frustrated with your final time. Use the MMs as reality checks on your current performance level, and remember that they are based upon "ideal conditions and training".

8. Speed repetitions of 2 miles each are listed on the schedule for this goal. During each 2 miler, run the first and the last 800 meters in 3:30, and run the mile in the middle in 6:50-6:55. At the one mile mark, walk for 20 seconds. Stay smooth. If you are struggling to maintain pace, slow down to run efficiently. If you are slowing down significantly during the second mile, shift to running twice as many one mile repeats. Be sure to read the section in this book on speed training.

9. Warm up for each 2 mile repeat workout by walking for 2-5 minutes, then jog very slowly for 5-10 minutes. Next, do 4-8 acceleration-gliders (see the segment about this in this book). Reverse this process as you warm down, leaving out the acceleration gliders.

10. Recover between each 2 mile repeat by walking and jogging for 5-6 minutes between each. You may choose the amount of walking vs. jogging. If you are using a heart monitor, your heart rate should drop below 65 % of max heart rate before starting another 2 mile repeat.

11. If you have recovered from the weekend run, during your Tuesday workout run 2-4 miles at race pace (noted as "p" on the Tue line). After an easy warm-up, run 4 of the acceleration-gliders (Acg). (These are described in the drill section of this book). Then run a mile segment at 7:25, take a 45 sec walk break, and run a second mile with a total time of 14:50, take another 40 sec walk break and continue for 1-2 more miles. This means that you will have to pick up the pace by a few seconds per minute to maintain your 7:25 pace by the watch. Stay smooth and try to maintain the same pace. This trains you to run at race pace, taking walk breaks.

12. It is fine to do cross training on Monday and Friday, if you wish. Except for running in the water, cross training doesn't tend to improve performance. Avoid exercises like spinning and stair machines (during rest days from running) that use the calf muscles.

13. Be sure to take a vacation from strenuous exercise the day before your long runs and 2 mile repetitions.

14. On Friday, run a few hill repeats (h), as described in the hill section in this book. The Acg's will get the legs warmed up for the hill accelerations. The length of the hills should be 250 meters to 350 meters. Walk down most of each hill for almost complete recovery.

15. Hills (h) are suggested on short mileage weekends, during the early weeks of the program. Start with 2 hill repeats and increase by one hill on each successive workout until you reach 5 hills, as noted on the schedule. Because Boston has some significant hills in strategic locations, these workouts are crucial. The hills are embedded into the total mileage for the day.

16. Double workouts can be run on Tuesday and Friday. See the chapter in this book called "For Extra Credit."

17. During the last two weeks of the program, you cannot improve performance so avoid running too fast. On some of the short mile days, however, it is OK to run a 2 mile segment running 7:25 pace, while taking a 45 second walk break at the mile mark. This fine-tunes your pace judgment and your mental focus.

18. Never run through pain—read the chapter on injuries if you sense that you have the beginning of an injury.

Mon	Tue (CDAcg/p)	Wed	Thurs (CD)	Fri (Acg/h)	Sat	Sun
Week 1						
off	45 min run	off or XT	30 min run	60 min	off	7 miles
Week 2						
off	45 min run	off/XT	30 min run	60 min	off	8 miles
Week 3						
off	50 min run	off/XT	30 min run	60 min	off	5 mi with 2 hills
Week 4						
off	50 min run	off/XT	30 min run	60 min	off	9.5 miles
Week 5						
off	40 min run	off/XT	30 min run	60 min	off	5 mi with 3 hills
Week 6						
off	50 min run	off/XT	30 min run	60 min	off	11 miles
Week 7						
off	40 min run	off/XT	30 min run	60 min	off	6 mi with 4 hills
Week 8						
off	55 min run	off/XT	30 min run	60 min	off	13 miles
Week 9						
off	40 min run	off/XT	30 min run	60 min	off	6 mi with 5 hills
Week 10						
off	55 min run	off/XT	30 min run	60 min	off	15 miles
Week 11						
off	40 min run	off/XT	30 min run	60 min	off	2 x 2 mile
Week 12						
off	60 min run	off/XT	30 min run	60 min	off	17 miles
Week 13						
off	40 min run	off/XT	30 min run	70 min	off	3 x 2 mile
Week 14						
off	60 min run	off/XT	30 min run	70 min	off	8 miles MM
Week 15						
off	65 min run	off/XT	30 min run	70 min	off	20 miles

Week 16						
off	45 min run	off/XT	30 min run	70 min	off	4 x 2 mile

Week 17						
off	65 min run	off/XT	30 min run	70 min	off	7 miles MM

Week 18						
off	65 min run	off/XT	30 min run	70 min	off	23 miles

Week 19						
off	45 min run	off/XT	30 min run	70 min	off	5 x 2 mile

Week 20						
off	70 min run	off/XT	30 min run	70 min	off	7 miles MM

Week 21						
off	70 min run	off/XT	30 min run	60 min	off	26 miles

Week 22						
off	45 min run	off/XT	30 min run	75 min	off	6 miles

Week 23						
off	70 min run	off/XT	30 min run	70 min	off	6 x 2 mile

Week 24						
off	70 min run	off/XT	30 min run	75 min	off	7 miles MM

Week 25						
off	70 min run	off/XT	30 min run	60 min	off	29 miles

Week 26						
off	70 min run	off/XT	30 min run	75 min	off	6 miles

Week 27						
off	70 min run	off/XT	30 min run	60 min	off	7 x 2 miles

Week 28						
off	45 min run	off/XT	30 min run	70 min	off	7 miles

Week 29						
off	40 min run	off/XT	30 min run	30 min	off	Goal Race/Boston

Week 30 (Recovery week)						
off/XT	30 min run	off/XT	30 min run	off	5 miles	off

Time goal 3:25

Note: This is the minimum that I've found necessary to prepare for the goal. If you are already running more than this amount, and are able to recover between workouts, you may continue to do what you are doing—but be careful.

1. To begin this program, you should have run a long run within the past 2 weeks of at least 6 miles. If your long run is not this long, then gradually increase the weekend run to this distance before starting the program.

2. If your current long run is longer than 7 miles, it is possible to start on the week with a long run that is at or slightly longer than the distance of the longest run you have run in the past 2 weeks. For example, if you ran 13 miles two weeks ago, you could start with week # 8, # 9 or # 10. In this case, you will lose the benefits from the hill workouts on the short mileage weekends.

3. What is your current level of performance? The "magic mile" time trials, noted by MM on the schedule, will tell you. Read the chapter in this book on "Choosing the Right Goal..." Take your current MM and multiply by 1.3. This predicts your best possible per mile performance in the marathon under ideal conditions when you've done all of the training. Follow the instructions in that chapter to set a realistic goal and to monitor your progress. The MM is run once on each weekend noted in the schedule. You can run any pace you wish for the remaining miles assigned on these workouts. To predict a 3:25 marathon performance, your MM should be 5:50 or faster by the end of the program.

4. What pace should I run on the long runs? Take your current performance level (MM x 1.3) and add 2 minutes. The result is your suggested long run pace per mile on long runs at 60F or cooler. For those who are currently predicting a 3:25 in the marathon, the long run pace should be no faster than 9:40 per mile at 60F and 10:40/mi at 70F. It is always better to run slower to ensure faster recovery.

5. On long runs, and in the marathon itself, slow down even more when the temperature rises: by 30 seconds a mile for every 5 degrees above 60F.

6. Run-Walk-Run ratio should correspond to the pace used (See the Run-Walk-Run chapter in this book).

7. Most runners don't improve more than 30 seconds per mile during a 30-week marathon training program. If your goal is more aggressive, you may increase injury stress during the training or may be frustrated with your final time. Use the MMs as reality checks on your current performance level, and remember that they are based upon "ideal projections."

8. Speed repetitions of 2 miles each are listed on the schedule for this goal. During each 2 miler, run the first and the last 800 meters in 3:35, and run the mile in the middle in 7:00 to 7:05. At the one mile mark, walk for 20 seconds. Stay smooth. If you are struggling to maintain pace, slow down to run efficiently. If you are slowing down significantly during the second mile, shift to running twice as many one mile repeats. Be sure to read the section in this book on speed training.

9. Warm up for each 2 mile repeat workout by walking for 2-5 minutes, then jog very slowly for 5-10 minutes. Next, do 4-8 acceleration-gliders (see the segment about this in this book). Reverse this process as you warm down, leaving out the acceleration gliders.

10. Recover between each 2 mile repeat by walking and jogging for 6 minutes between each. You may choose the amount of walking vs. jogging. If you are using a heart monitor, your heart rate should drop below 65 % of max heart rate before starting another 2 mile repeat.

11. If you have recovered from the weekend run, during your Tuesday workout run 2-4 miles at race pace (noted as "p" on the Tue line). After an easy warm-up, run 4 of the acceleration-gliders (Acg). (These are described in the drill section of this book). Then run a mile segment at 7:36, and run a second mile with a total time of 15:12, and continue at the same pace per mile for 1-2 more miles. From the beginning of these segments, take a 25 second walk break after 4 minutes of running. This means that you will have to pick up the pace by a few seconds per minute to maintain your 7:36 pace by the watch. Stay smooth and try to maintain the same pace. This trains you to run at race pace, taking walk breaks.

12. It is fine to do cross training on Monday and Friday, if you wish. Except for running in the water, cross training doesn't tend to improve performance. Avoid exercises like stair machines (during rest days from running) that use the calf muscles.

13. Be sure to take a vacation from strenuous exercise the day before your long runs and mile repetitions.

14. On Friday, run a few hill repeats (h), as described in the hill section in this book. The Acg's will get the legs warmed up for the hill accelerations. The length of the hills should be 250 meters to 350 meters. Walk down most of each hill for almost complete recovery.

15. Hills (h) are suggested on short mileage weekends, during the early weeks of the program. Start with 2 hill repeats and increase by one hill on each successive workout until you reach 5 hills, as noted on the schedule. Because Boston has some significant hills in strategic locations, these workouts are crucial. The hills are embedded into the total mileage for the day.

16. Double workouts can be run on Tuesday and Friday. See the chapter in this book called "For Extra Credit."

17. During the last two weeks of the program, you cannot improve performance so avoid running too fast. On some of the short mile days, however, it is OK to run a 2 mile segment running 7:36 pace, while taking a 25 second walk break after each 4 minutes of running. This fine-tunes your pace judgment and your mental focus.

18. Never run through pain—read the chapter on injuries if you sense that you have the beginning of an injury.

Mon	Tue (CDAcg/p)	Wed	Thurs (CD)	Fri (Acg/h)	Sat	Sun
Week 1						
off	45 min run	off or XT	30 min run	60 min	off	7 miles
Week 2						
off	45 min run	off/XT	30 min run	60 min	off	8 miles
Week 3						
off	50 min run	off/XT	30 min run	60 min	off	5 mi with 2 hills
Week 4						
off	50 min run	off/XT	30 min run	60 min	off	9.5 miles
Week 5						
off	40 min run	off/XT	30 min run	60 min	off	5 mi with 3 hills
Week 6						
off	50 min run	off/XT	30 min run	60 min	off	11 miles
Week 7						
off	40 min run	off/XT	30 min run	60 min	off	6 mi with 4 hills
Week 8						
off	55 min run	off/XT	30 min run	60 min	off	13 miles
Week 9						
off	40 min run	off/XT	30 min run	60 min	off	6 mi with 5 hills
Week 10						
off	55 min run	off/XT	30 min run	60 min	off	15 miles
Week 11						
off	40 min run	off/XT	30 min run	60 min	off	2 x 2 mile
Week 12						
off	60 min run	off/XT	30 min run	60 min	off	17 miles
Week 13						
off	40 min run	off/XT	30 min run	60 min	off	3 x 2 mile
Week 14						
off	60 min run	off/XT	30 min run	60 min	off	8 miles MM
Week 15						
off	65 min run	off/XT	30 min run	60 min	off	20 miles

Week 16

off	45 min run	off/XT	30 min run	60 min	off	4 x 2 mile

Week 17

off	65 min run	off/XT	30 min run	70 min	off	7 miles MM

Week 18

off	65 min run	off/XT	30 min run	60 min	off	23 miles

Week 19

off	45 min run	off/XT	30 min run	70 min	off	5 x 2 mile

Week 20

off	70 min run	off/XT	30 min run	70 min	off	7 miles MM

Week 21

off	70 min run	off/XT	30 min run	60 min	off	26 miles

Week 22

off	45 min run	off/XT	30 min run	70 min	off	6 miles

Week 23

off	70 min run	off/XT	30 min run	70 min	off	6 x 2 mile

Week 24

off	70 min run	off/XT	30 min run	70 min	off	7 miles MM

Week 25

off	70 min run	off/XT	30 min run	60 min	off	29 miles

Week 26

off	70 min run	off/XT	30 min run	70 min	off	6 miles

Week 27

off	70 min run	off/XT	30 min run	60 min	off	7 x 2 miles

Week 28

off	45 min run	off/XT	30 min run	60 min	off	7 miles

Week 29

off	40 min run	off/XT	30 min run	30 min	off	Goal Race/Boston

Week 30 (Recovery week)

off/XT	30 min run	off/XT	30 min run	off	5 miles	off

Time goal 3:30

Note: This is the minimum that I've found necessary to prepare for the goal. If you are already running more than this amount, and are able to recover between workouts, you may continue to do what you are doing—but be careful.

1. To begin this program, you should have run a long run within the past 2 weeks of at least 6 miles. If your long run is not this long, then gradually increase the weekend run to this distance before starting the program.

2. If your current long run is longer than 7 miles, it is possible to start on the week with a long run that is at or slightly longer than the distance of the longest run you have run in the past 2 weeks. For example, if you ran 13 miles two weeks ago, you could start with week # 8, # 9 or # 10. In this case, you will lose the benefits from the hill workouts on the short mileage weekends.

3. What is your current level of performance? The "magic mile" time trials, noted by MM on the schedule, will tell you. Read the chapter in this book on "Choosing the Right Goal..." Take your current MM and multiply by 1.3. This predicts your best possible per mile performance in the marathon under ideal conditions when you've done all of the training. Follow the instructions in that chapter to set a realistic goal and to monitor your progress. The MM is run once on each weekend noted in the schedule. You can run any pace you wish for the remaining miles assigned on these workouts. To predict a 3:30 marathon performance, your MM should be 6:05 or faster by the end of the program.

4. What pace should I run on the long runs? Take your current performance level (MM x 1.3) and add 2 minutes. The result is your suggested long run pace per mile on long runs at 60F or cooler. For those who are currently predicting a 3:30 in the marathon, the long run pace should be no faster than 10 min/mile at 60F and 11 min/mi at 70F. It is always better to run slower to ensure faster recovery.

5. On long runs, and in the marathon itself, slow down even more when the temperature rises: by 30 seconds a mile for every 5 degrees above 60F.

6. Run-Walk-Run ratio should correspond to the pace used (See the Run-Walk-Run chapter in this book).

7. Most runners don't improve more than 30 seconds per mile during a 30-week marathon training program. If your goal is more aggressive, you may increase injury stress during the training or may be frustrated with your final time. Use the MMs as reality checks on your current performance level, and remember that they are based upon "ideal projections."

8. Speed repetitions of 2 miles each are listed on the schedule for this goal. During each 2 miler, run the first and the last 800 meters in 3:50, and run the mile in the middle in 7:20-25. After each 800 meter, walk for 15 seconds. Stay smooth. If you are struggling to maintain pace, slow down to run efficiently. If you are slowing down significantly during the second mile, shift to running twice as many one mile repeats. Be sure to read the section in this book on speed training.

9. Warm up for each 2 mile repeat workout by walking for 2-5 minutes, then jog very slowly for 5-10 minutes. Next, do 4-8 acceleration-gliders (see the segment about this in this book). Reverse this process as you warm down, leaving out the acceleration gliders.

10. Recover between each 2 mile repeat by walking and jogging for 6 minutes between each. You may choose the amount of walking vs. jogging. If you are using a heart monitor, your heart rate should drop below 65 % of max heart rate before starting another 2 mile repeat.

11. If you have recovered from the weekend run, during your Tuesday workout run 2-4 miles at race pace (noted as "p" on the Tue line). After an easy warm-up, run 4 of the acceleration-gliders (Acg). (These are described in the drill section of this book). Then run a mile segment at 8:00, and run a second mile with a total time of 16:00, and continue at the same pace per mile for 1-2 more miles. From the beginning of these segments, take a 30 second walk break after 4 minutes of running. This means that you will have to pick up the pace by a few seconds per minute to maintain your 8:00 pace by the watch. Stay smooth and try to maintain the same pace. This trains you to run at race pace, taking walk breaks.

12. It is fine to do cross training on Monday and Friday, if you wish. Except for running in the water, cross training doesn't tend to improve performance. Avoid exercises like stair machines (during rest days from running) that use the calf muscles.

13. Be sure to take a vacation from strenuous exercise the day before your long runs and mile repetitions.

14. On Friday, run a few hill repeats (h), as described in the hill section in this book. The Acg's will get the legs warmed up for the hill accelerations. The length of the hills should be 200 meters to 300 meters. Walk down most of each hill for almost complete recovery.

15. Hills (h) are suggested on short mileage weekends, during the early weeks of the program. Start with 2 hill repeats and increase by one hill on each successive workout until you reach 5 hills, as noted on the schedule. Because Boston has some significant hills in strategic locations, these workouts are crucial. The hills are embedded into the total mileage for the day.

16. Double workouts can be run on Tuesday and Friday. See the chapter in this book called "For Extra Credit."

17. During the last two weeks of the program, you cannot improve performance so avoid running too fast. On some of the short mile days, however, it is OK to run a 2 mile segment running 8:00 pace, while taking a 30 second walk break after each 4 minutes of running. This fine-tunes your pace judgment and your mental focus.

18. Never run through pain—read the chapter on injuries if you sense that you have the beginning of an injury.

Mon	Tue (CDAcg/p)	Wed	Thurs (CD)	Fri (Acg/h)	Sat	Sun
Week 1						
off	45 min run	off or XT	30 min run	40 min	off	7 miles
Week 2						
off	45 min run	off/XT	30 min run	40 min	off	8 miles
Week 3						
off	50 min run	off/XT	30 min run	40 min	off	5 mi with 2 hills
Week 4						
off	50 min run	off/XT	30 min run	40 min	off	9.5 miles
Week 5						
off	40 min run	off/XT	30 min run	45 min	off	5 mi with 3 hills
Week 6						
off	50 min run	off/XT	30 min run	45 min	off	11 miles
Week 7						
off	40 min run	off/XT	30 min run	45 min	off	6 mi with 4 hills
Week 8						
off	55 min run	off/XT	30 min run	45 min	off	13 miles
Week 9						
off	40 min run	off/XT	30 min run	50 min	off	6 mi with 5 hills
Week 10						
off	55 min run	off/XT	30 min run	50 min	off	15 miles
Week 11						
off	40 min run	off/XT	30 min run	50 min	off	2 x 2 mile
Week 12						
off	60 min run	off/XT	30 min run	50 min	off	17 miles
Week 13						
off	40 min run	off/XT	30 min run	60 min	off	3 x 2 mile
Week 14						
off	60 min run	off/XT	30 min run	60 min	off	8 miles MM
Week 15						
off	65 min run	off/XT	30 min run	60 min	off	20 miles

Week 16						
off	45 min run	off/XT	30 min run	50 min	off	4 x 2 mile
Week 17						
off	65 min run	off/XT	30 min run	70 min	off	7 miles MM
Week 18						
off	65 min run	off/XT	30 min run	60 min	off	23 miles
Week 19						
off	45 min run	off/XT	30 min run	60 min	off	5 x 2 mile
Week 20						
off	70 min run	off/XT	30 min run	70 min	off	7 miles MM
Week 21						
off	70 min run	off/XT	30 min run	60 min	off	26 miles
Week 22						
off	45 min run	off/XT	30 min run	70 min	off	6 miles
Week 23						
off	70 min run	off/XT	30 min run	60 min	off	6 x 2 mile
Week 24						
off	70 min run	off/XT	30 min run	70 min	off	7 miles MM
Week 25						
off	70 min run	off/XT	30 min run	60 min	off	29 miles
Week 26						
off	70 min run	off/XT	30 min run 7	0 min	off	6 miles
Week 27						
off	70 min run	off/XT	30 min run	60 min	off	7 x 2 miles
Week 28						
off	45 min run	off/XT	30 min run	60 min	off	7 miles
Week 29						
off	40 min run	off/XT	30 min run	30 min	off	Goal Race/Boston
Week 30 (Recovery week)						
off/XT	30 min run	off/XT	30 min run	off	5 miles	Marathon

Time goal 3:35

Note: This is the minimum that I've found necessary to prepare for the goal. If you are already running more than this amount, and are able to recover between workouts, you may continue to do what you are doing—but be careful.

1. To begin this program, you should have run a long run within the past 2 weeks of at least 6 miles. If your long run is not this long, then gradually increase the weekend run to this distance before starting the program.

2. If your current long run is longer than 7 miles, it is possible to start on the week with a long run that is at or slightly longer than the distance of the longest run you have run in the past 2 weeks. For example, if you ran 13 miles two weeks ago, you could start with week # 8, # 9 or # 10. In this case, you will lose the benefits from the hill workouts on the short mileage weekends.

3. What is your current level of performance? The "magic mile" time trials, noted by MM on the schedule, will tell you. Read the chapter in this book on "Choosing the Right Goal..." Take your current MM and multiply by 1.3. This predicts your best possible per mile performance in the marathon under ideal conditions when you've done all of the training. Follow the instructions in that chapter to set a realistic goal and to monitor your progress. The MM is run once on each weekend noted in the schedule. You can run any pace you wish for the remaining miles assigned on these workouts. To predict a 3:35 marathon performance, your MM should be 6:15 or faster by the end of the program.

4. What pace should I run on the long runs? Take your current performance level (MM x 1.3) and add 2 minutes. The result is your suggested long run pace per mile on long runs at 60F or cooler. For those who are currently predicting a 3:35 in the marathon, the long run pace should be no faster than 10:15 min/mile at 60F and 11:15 min/mi at 70F. It is always better to run slower to ensure faster recovery.

5. On long runs, and in the marathon itself, slow down even more when the temperature rises: by 30 seconds a mile for every 5 degrees above 60F.

6. Run-Walk-Run ratio should correspond to the pace used (See the Run-Walk-Run chapter in this book).

7. Most runners don't improve more than 30 seconds per mile during a 30-week marathon training program. If your goal is more aggressive, you may increase injury stress during the training or may be frustrated with your final time. Use the MMs as reality checks on your current performance level, and remember that they are based upon "ideal projections."

8. Speed repetitions of 2 miles each are listed on the schedule for this goal. During each 2 miler, run the first and the last 800 meters in 4:00, and run the mile in the middle in 7:40-45. After each 800 meter, walk for 20 seconds. Stay smooth. If you are struggling to maintain pace, slow down to run efficiently. If you are

slowing down significantly during the second mile, shift to running twice as many one mile repeats. Be sure to read the section in this book on speed training.

9. Warm up for each 2 mile repeat workout by walking for 2-5 minutes, then jog very slowly for 5-10 minutes. Next, do 4-8 acceleration-gliders (see the segment about this in this book). Reverse this process as you warm down, leaving out the acceleration gliders.

10. Recover between each mile repeat by walking and jogging for 6 minutes between each. You may choose the amount of walking vs. jogging. If you are using a heart monitor, your heart rate should drop below 65 % of max heart rate before starting another mile repeat.

11. If you have recovered from the weekend run, during your Tuesday workout run 2-4 miles at race pace (noted as "p" on the Tue line). After an easy warm-up, run 4 of the acceleration-gliders (Acg). (These are described in the drill section of this book). Then run a mile segment at 8:12, and run a second mile with a total time of 16:24, and continue at the same pace per mile for 1-2 more miles. From the beginning of these segments, take a 35 second walk break after 4 minutes of running. This means that you will have to pick up the pace by a few seconds per minute to maintain your 8:12 pace by the watch. Stay smooth and try to maintain the same pace. This trains you to run at race pace, taking walk breaks.

12. It is fine to do cross training on Monday and Friday, if you wish. Except for running in the water, cross training doesn't tend to improve performance. Avoid exercises like stair machines (during rest days from running) that use the calf muscles.

13. Be sure to take a vacation from strenuous exercise the day before your long runs and mile repetitions.

14. On Friday, run a few hill repeats (h), as described in the hill section in this book. The Acg's will get the legs warmed up for the hill accelerations. The length of the hills should be 200 meters to 300 meters. Walk down most of each hill for almost complete recovery.

15. Hills (h) are suggested on short mileage weekends, during the early weeks of the program. Start with 2 hill repeats and increase by one hill on each successive workout until you reach 5 hills, as noted on the schedule. Because Boston has some significant hills in strategic locations, these workouts are crucial. The hills are embedded into the total mileage for the day.

16. Double workouts can be run on Tuesday and Friday. See the chapter in this book called "For Extra Credit."

17. During the last two weeks of the program, you cannot improve performance so avoid running too fast. On some of the short mile days, however, it is OK to run a 2 mile segment running 8:12 pace, while taking a 35 second walk break after each 4 minutes of running. This fine-tunes your pace judgment and your mental focus.

18. Never run through pain—read the chapter on injuries if you sense that you have the beginning of an injury.

Mon	Tue (CDAcg/p)	Wed	Thurs (CD)	Fri (Acg/h)	Sat	Sun
Week 1						
off	45 min run	off or XT	30 min run	40 min	off	7 miles
Week 2						
off	45 min run	off/XT	30 min run	40 min	off	8 miles
Week 3						
off	50 min run	off/XT	30 min run	40 min	off	5 mi with 2 hills
Week 4						
off	50 min run	off/XT	30 min run	40 min	off	9.5 miles
Week 5						
off	40 min run	off/XT	30 min run	45 min	off	5 mi with 3 hills
Week 6						
off	50 min run	off/XT	30 min run	45 min	off	11 miles
Week 7						
off	40 min run	off/XT	30 min run	45 min	off	6 mi with 4 hills
Week 8						
off	55 min run	off/XT	30 min run	45 min	off	13 miles
Week 9						
off	40 min run	off/XT	30 min run	50 min	off	6 mi with 5 hills
Week 10						
off	55 min run	off/XT	30 min run	50 min	off	15 miles
Week 11						
off	40 min run	off/XT	30 min run	50 min	off	2 x 2 mile
Week 12						
off	60 min run	off/XT	30 min run	50 min	off	17 miles
Week 13						
off	40 min run	off/XT	30 min run	60 min	off	3 x 2 mile
Week 14						
off	60 min run	off/XT	30 min run	60 min	off	8 miles MM
Week 15						
off	65 min run	off/XT	30 min run	60 min	off	20 miles

Week 16						
off	45 min run	off/XT	30 min run	50 min	off	4 x 2 mile

Week 17						
off	65 min run	off/XT	30 min run	70 min	off	7 miles MM

Week 18						
off	65 min run	off/XT	30 min run	60 min	off	23 miles

Week 19						
off	45 min run	off/XT	30 min run	60 min	off	5 x 2 mile

Week 20						
off	70 min run	off/XT	30 min run	70 min	off	7 miles MM

Week 21						
off	70 min run	off/XT	30 min run	60 min	off	26 miles

Week 22						
off	45 min run	off/XT	30 min run	70 min	off	6 miles

Week 23						
off	70 min run	off/XT	30 min run	60 min	off	6 x 2 mile

Week 24						
off	70 min run	off/XT	30 min run	70 min	off	7 miles MM

Week 25						
off	70 min run	off/XT	30 min run	60 min	off	29 miles

Week 26						
off	70 min run	off/XT	30 min run	70 min	off	6 miles

Week 27						
off	70 min run	off/XT	30 min run	60 min	off	7 x 2 miles

Week 28						
off	45 min run	off/XT	30 min run	60 min	off	7 miles

Week 29						
off	40 min run	off/XT	30 min run	30 min	off	Goal Race/Boston

Week 30 (Recovery week)						
off/XT	30 min run	off/XT	30 min run	off	5 miles	off

Time goal 3:40

Note: This is the minimum that I've found necessary to prepare for the goal. If you are already running more than this amount, and are able to recover between workouts, you may continue to do what you are doing—but be careful.

1. To begin this program, you should have run a long run within the past 2 weeks of at least 6 miles. If your long run is not this long, then gradually increase the weekend run to this distance before starting the program.

2. If your current long run is longer than 7 miles, it is possible to start on the week with a long run that is at or slightly longer than the distance of the longest run you have run in the past 2 weeks. For example, if you ran 13 miles two weeks ago, you could start with week # 8, # 9 or # 10. In this case, you will lose the benefits from the hill workouts on the short mileage weekends.

3. What is your current level of performance? The "magic mile" time trials, noted by MM on the schedule, will tell you. Read the chapter in this book on "Choosing the Right Goal..." Take your current MM and multiply by 1.3. This predicts your best possible per mile performance in the marathon under ideal conditions when you've done all of the training. Follow the instructions in that chapter to set a realistic goal and to monitor your progress. The MM is run once on each weekend noted in the schedule. You can run any pace you wish for the remaining miles assigned on these workouts. To predict a 3:40 marathon performance, your MM should be 6:22 or faster by the end of the program.

4. What pace should I run on the long runs? Take your current performance level (MM x 1.3) and add 2 minutes. The result is your suggested long run pace per mile on long runs at 60F or cooler. For those who are currently predicting a 3:40 in the marathon, the long run pace should be no faster than 10:30/mile at 60F and 11:30/mi at 70F. It is always better to run slower to ensure faster recovery.

5. On long runs, and in the marathon itself, slow down even more when the temperature rises: by 30 seconds a mile for every 5 degrees above 60F.

6. Run-Walk-Run ratio should correspond to the pace used (See the Run-Walk-Run chapter in this book).

7. Most runners don't improve more than 30 seconds per mile during a 30-week marathon training program. If your goal is more aggressive, you may increase injury stress during the training or may be frustrated with your final time. Use the MMs as reality checks on your current performance level, and remember that they are based upon "ideal projections."

8. Speed repetitions of 2 miles each are listed on the schedule for this goal. During each 2 miler, run the first and the last 800 meters in 4:00, and run the mile in the middle in 7:50. After each 800 meter, walk for 15 seconds. Stay smooth. If you are struggling to maintain pace, slow down to run efficiently. If you are slowing down significantly during the second mile, shift to running twice as many one mile repeats. Be sure to read the section in this book on speed training.

9. Warm up for each 2 mile repeat workout by walking for 2-5 minutes, then jog very slowly for 5-10 minutes. Next, do 4-8 acceleration-gliders (see the segment about this in this book). Reverse this process as you warm down, leaving out the acceleration gliders.

10. Recover between each 2 mile repeat by walking and jogging for 6 minutes between each. You may choose the amount of walking vs. jogging. If you are using a heart monitor, your heart rate should drop below 65 % of max heart rate before starting another 2 mile repeat.

11. If you have recovered from the weekend run, during your Tuesday workout run 2-4 miles at race pace (noted as "p" on the Tue line). After an easy warm-up, run 4 of the acceleration-gliders (Acg). (These are described in the drill section of this book). Then run a mile segment at 8:22, and run a second mile with a total time of 16:44, and continue at the same pace per mile for 1-2 more miles. From the beginning of these segments, take a 40 second walk break after 4 minutes of running. This means that you will have to pick up the pace by a few seconds per minute to maintain your 8:22 pace by the watch. Stay smooth and try to maintain the same pace. This trains you to run at race pace, taking walk breaks.

12. It is fine to do cross training on Monday and Friday, if you wish. Except for running in the water, cross training doesn't tend to improve performance. Avoid exercises like stair machines (during rest days from running) that use the calf muscles.

13. Be sure to take a vacation from strenuous exercise the day before your long runs and mile repetitions.

14. On Friday, run a few hill repeats (h), as described in the hill section in this book. The Acg's will get the legs warmed up for the hill accelerations. The length of the hills should be 200 meters to 300 meters. Walk down most of each hill for almost complete recovery.

15. Hills (h) are suggested on short mileage weekends, during the early weeks of the program. Start with 2 hill repeats and increase by one hill on each successive workout until you reach 5 hills, as noted on the schedule. Because Boston has some significant hills in strategic locations, these workouts are crucial. The hills are embedded into the total mileage for the day.

16. Double workouts can be run on Tuesday and Friday. See the chapter in this book called "For Extra Credit."

17. During the last two weeks of the program, you cannot improve performance so avoid running too fast. On some of the short mile days, however, it is OK to run a 2 mile segment running 8:22 pace, while taking a 40 second walk break after each 4 minutes of running. This fine-tunes your pace judgment and your mental focus.

18. Never run through pain—read the chapter on injuries if you sense that you have the beginning of an injury.

Mon	Tue (CDAcg/p)	Wed	Thurs (CD)	Fri (Acg/h)	Sat	Sun
Week 1						
off	45 min run	off or XT	30 min run	40 min	off	7 miles
Week 2						
off	45 min run	off/XT	30 min run	40 min	off	8 miles
Week 3						
off	50 min run	off/XT	30 min run	40 min	off	5 mi with 2 hills
Week 4						
off	50 min run	off/XT	30 min run	40 min	off	9.5 miles
Week 5						
off	40 min run	off/XT	30 min run	45 min	off	5 mi with 3 hills
Week 6						
off	50 min run	off/XT	30 min run	45 min	off	11 miles
Week 7						
off	40 min run	off/XT	30 min run	45 min	off	6 mi with 4 hills
Week 8						
off	55 min run	off/XT	30 min run	45 min	off	13 miles
Week 9						
off	40 min run	off/XT	30 min run	50 min	off	6 mi with 5 hills
Week 10						
off	55 min run	off/XT	30 min run	50 min	off	15 miles
Week 11						
off	40 min run	off/XT	30 min run	50 min	off	2 x 2 mile
Week 12						
off	60 min run	off/XT	30 min run	50 min	off	17 miles
Week 13						
off	40 min run	off/XT	30 min run	60 min	off	3 x 2 mile
Week 14						
off	60 min run	off/XT	30 min run	60 min	off	8 miles MM
Week 15						
off	65 min run	off/XT	30 min run	60 min	off	20 miles

Week 16

off	45 min run	off/XT	30 min run	50 min	off	4 x 2 mile

Week 17

off	65 min run	off/XT	30 min run	70 min	off	7 miles MM

Week 18

off	65 min run	off/XT	30 min run	60 min	off	23 miles

Week 19

off	45 min run	off/XT	30 min run	60 min	off	5 x 2 mile

Week 20

off	70 min run	off/XT	30 min run	70 min	off	7 miles MM

Week 21

off	70 min run	off/XT	30 min run	60 min	off	26 miles

Week 22

off	45 min run	off/XT	30 min run	70 min	off	6 miles

Week 23

off	70 min run	off/XT	30 min run	60 min	off	6 x 2 mile

Week 24

off	70 min run	off/XT	30 min run	70 min	off	7 miles MM

Week 25

off	70 min run	off/XT	30 min run	60 min	off	29 miles

Week 26

off	70 min run	off/XT	30 min run	70 min	off	6 miles

Week 27

off	70 min run	off/XT	30 min run	60 min	off	7 x 2 miles

Week 28

off	45 min run	off/XT	30 min run	60 min	off	7 miles

Week 29

off	40 min run	off/XT	30 min run	30 min	off	Goal Race/Boston

Week 30 (Recovery week)

off/XT	30 min run	off/XT	30 min run	off	5 miles	off

Time goal 3:45

Note: This is the minimum that I've found necessary to prepare for the goal. If you are already running more than this amount, and are able to recover between workouts, you may continue to do what you are doing—but be careful.

1. To begin this program, you should have run a long run within the past 2 weeks of at least 6 miles. If your long run is not this long, then gradually increase the weekend run to this distance before starting the program.

2. If your current long run is longer than 7 miles, it is possible to start on the week with a long run that is at or slightly longer than the distance of the longest run you have run in the past 2 weeks. For example, if you ran 13 miles two weeks ago, you could start with week # 8, # 9 or # 10. In this case, you will lose the benefits from the hill workouts on the short mileage weekends.

3. What is your current level of performance? The "magic mile" time trials, noted by MM on the schedule, will tell you. Read the chapter in this book on "Choosing the Right Goal..." Take your current MM and multiply by 1.3. This predicts your best possible per mile performance in the marathon under ideal conditions when you've done all of the training. Follow the instructions in that chapter to set a realistic goal and to monitor your progress. The MM is run once on each weekend noted in the schedule. You can run any pace you wish for the remaining miles assigned on these workouts. To predict a 3:45 marathon performance, your MM should be 6:35 or faster by the end of the program.

4. What pace should I run on the long runs? Take your current performance level (MM x 1.3) and add 2 minutes. The result is your suggested long run pace per mile on long runs at 60F or cooler. For those who are currently predicting a 3:45 in the marathon, the long run pace should be no faster than 10:40/mile at 60F and 11:40/mi at 70F. It is always better to run slower to ensure faster recovery.

5. On long runs, and in the marathon itself, slow down even more when the temperature rises: by 30 seconds a mile for every 5 degrees above 60F.

6. Run-Walk-Run ratio should correspond to the pace used (See the Run-Walk-Run chapter in this book).

7. Most runners don't improve more than 30 seconds per mile during a 30-week marathon training program. If your goal is more aggressive, you may increase injury stress during the training or may be frustrated with your final time. Use the MMs as reality checks on your current performance level, and remember that they are based upon "ideal projections."

8. Speed repetitions of 2 miles each are listed on the schedule for this goal. During each 2 miler, run the first and the last 800 meters in 4:10, and run the mile in the middle in 8:00. After each 800 meter, walk for 15 seconds. Stay smooth. If you are struggling to maintain pace, slow down to run efficiently. If you are slowing down significantly during the second mile, shift to running twice as many one mile repeats. Be sure to read the section in this book on speed training.

9. Warm up for each 2 mile repeat workout by walking for 2-5 minutes, then jog very slowly for 5-10 minutes. Next, do 4-8 acceleration-gliders (see the segment about this in this book). Reverse this process as you warm down, leaving out the acceleration gliders.

10. Recover between each 2 mile repeat by walking and jogging for 7 minutes between each. You may choose the amount of walking vs. jogging. If you are using a heart monitor, your heart rate should drop below 65 % of max heart rate before starting another 2 mile repeat.

11. If you have recovered from the weekend run, during your Tuesday workout run 2-4 miles at race pace (noted as "p" on the Tue line). After an easy warm-up, run 4 of the acceleration-gliders (Acg). (These are described in the drill section of this book). Then run a mile segment at 8:30, and run a second mile with a total time of 17:04, and continue at the same pace per mile for 1-2 more miles. From the beginning of these segments, take a 45 second walk break after 4 minutes of running. This means that you will have to pick up the pace by a few seconds per minute to maintain your 8:30 pace by the watch. Stay smooth and try to maintain the same pace. This trains you to run at race pace, taking walk breaks.

12. It is fine to do cross training on Monday and Friday, if you wish. Except for running in the water, cross training doesn't tend to improve performance. Avoid exercises like stair machines (during rest days from running) that use the calf muscles.

13. Be sure to take a vacation from strenuous exercise the day before your long runs and mile repetitions.

14. On Friday, run a few hill repeats (h), as described in the hill section in this book. The Acg's will get the legs warmed up for the hill accelerations. The length of the hills should be 200 meters to 300 meters. Walk down most of each hill for almost complete recovery.

15. Hills (h) are suggested on short mileage weekends, during the early weeks of the program. Start with 2 hill repeats and increase by one hill on each successive workout until you reach 5 hills, as noted on the schedule. Because Boston has some significant hills in strategic locations, these workouts are crucial. The hills are embedded into the total mileage for the day.

16. Double workouts can be run on Tuesday and Friday. See the chapter in this book called "For Extra Credit."

17. During the last two weeks of the program, you cannot improve performance so avoid running too fast. On some of the short mile days, however, it is OK to run a 2 mile segment running 8:30 pace, while taking a 45 second walk break after each 4 minutes of running. This fine-tunes your pace judgment and your mental focus.

18. Never run through pain—read the chapter on injuries if you sense that you have the beginning of an injury.

Mon	Tue (CDAcg/p)	Wed	Thurs (CD)	Fri (Acg/h)	Sat	Sun
Week 1						
off	45 min run	off or XT	30 min run	40 min	off	7 miles
Week 2						
off	45 min run	off/XT	30 min run	40 min	off	8 miles
Week 3						
off	50 min run	off/XT	30 min run	40 min	off	5 mi with 2 hills
Week 4						
off	50 min run	off/XT	30 min run	40 min	off	9.5 miles
Week 5						
off	40 min run	off/XT	30 min run	45 min	off	5 mi with 3 hills
Week 6						
off	50 min run	off/XT	30 min run	45 min	off	11 miles
Week 7						
off	40 min run	off/XT	30 min run	45 min	off	6 mi with 4 hills
Week 8						
off	55 min run	off/XT	30 min run	45 min	off	13 miles
Week 9						
off	40 min run	off/XT	30 min run	50 min	off	6 mi with 5 hills
Week 10						
off	55 min run	off/XT	30 min run	50 min	off	15 miles
Week 11						
off	40 min run	off/XT	30 min run	50 min	off	2 x 2 mile
Week 12						
off	60 min run	off/XT	30 min run	50 min	off	17 miles
Week 13						
off	40 min run	off/XT	30 min run	60 min	off	3 x 2 mile
Week 14						
off	60 min run	off/XT	30 min run	60 min	off	8 miles MM
Week 15						
off	65 min run	off/XT	30 min run	60 min	off	20 miles

Week 16						
off	45 min run	off/XT	30 min run	50 min	off	4 x 2 mile

Week 17						
off	65 min run	off/XT	30 min run	65 min	off	7 miles MM

Week 18						
off	65 min run	off/XT	30 min run	60 min	off	23 miles

Week 19						
off	45 min run	off/XT	30 min run	60 min	off	5 x 2 mile

Week 20						
off	65 min run	off/XT	30 min run	65 min	off	7 miles MM

Week 21						
off	65 min run	off/XT	30 min run	60 min	off	26 miles

Week 22						
off	45 min run	off/XT	30 min run	65 min	off	6 miles

Week 23						
off	65 min run	off/XT	30 min run	60 min	off	6 x 2 mile

Week 24						
off	65 min run	off/XT	30 min run	65 min	off	7 miles MM

Week 25						
off	65 min run	off/XT	30 min run	60 min	off	29 miles

Week 26						
off	65 min run	off/XT	30 min run	65 min	off	6 miles

Week 27						
off	65 min run	off/XT	30 min run	60 min	off	7 x 2 miles

Week 28						
off	45 min run	off/XT	30 min run	60 min	off	7 miles

Week 29						
off	40 min run	off/XT	30 min run	30 min	off	Goal Race/Boston

Week 30 (Recovery week)						
off/XT	30 min run	off/XT	30 min run	off	5 miles	off

Time goal 3:55

Note: This is the minimum that I've found necessary to prepare for the goal. If you are already running more than this amount, and are able to recover between workouts, you may continue to do what you are doing—but be careful.

1. To begin this program, you should have run a long run within the past 2 weeks of at least 6 miles. If your long run is not this long, then gradually increase the weekend run to this distance before starting the program.
2. If your current long run is longer than 7 miles, it is possible to start on the week with a long run that is at or slightly longer than the distance of the longest run you have run in the past 2 weeks. For example, if you ran 13 miles two weeks ago, you could start with week # 8, # 9 or # 10. In this case, you will lose the benefits from the hill workouts on the short mileage weekends.
3. What is your current level of performance? The "magic mile" time trials, noted by MM on the schedule, will tell you. Read the chapter in this book on "Choosing the Right Goal..." Take your current MM and multiply by 1.3. This predicts your best possible per mile performance in the marathon under ideal conditions when you've done all of the training. Follow the instructions in that chapter to set a realistic goal and to monitor your progress. The MM is run once on each weekend noted in the schedule. You can run any pace you wish for the remaining miles assigned on these workouts. To predict a 3:55 marathon performance, your MM should be 6:48 or faster by the end of the program.
4. What pace should I run on the long runs? Take your current performance level (MM x 1.3) and add 2 minutes. The result is your suggested long run pace per mile on long runs at 60F or cooler. For those who are currently predicting a 3:55 in the marathon, the long run pace should be no faster than 10:50/mile at 60F and 11:50/mi at 70F. It is always better to run slower to ensure faster recovery.
5. On long runs, and in the marathon itself, slow down even more when the temperature rises: by 30 seconds a mile for every 5 degrees above 60F.
6. Run-Walk-Run ratio should correspond to the pace used (See the Run-Walk-Run chapter in this book).
7. Most runners don't improve more than 30 seconds per mile during a 30-week marathon training program. If your goal is more aggressive, you may increase injury stress during the training or may be frustrated with your final time. Use the MMs as reality checks on your current performance level, and remember that they are based upon "ideal projections."
8. Speed repetitions of 2 miles each are listed on the schedule for this goal. During each 2 miler, run the first and the last 800 meters in 4:18, and run the mile in the middle in 8:10. After each 800 meter, walk for 20 seconds. Stay smooth. If you are struggling to maintain pace, slow down to run efficiently. If you are slowing down significantly during the second mile, shift to running twice as many one mile repeats. Be sure to read the section in this book on speed training.

9. Warm up for each 2 mile repeat workout by walking for 2-5 minutes, then jog very slowly for 5-10 minutes. Next, do 4-8 acceleration-gliders (see the segment about this in this book). Reverse this process as you warm down, leaving out the acceleration gliders.

10. Recover between each 2 mile repeat by walking and jogging for 7 minutes between each. You may choose the amount of walking vs. jogging. If you are using a heart monitor, your heart rate should drop below 65 % of max heart rate before starting another 2 mile repeat.

11. If you have recovered from the weekend run, during your Tuesday workout run 2-4 miles at race pace (noted as "p" on the Tue line). After an easy warm-up, run 4 of the acceleration-gliders (Acg). (These are described in the drill section of this book). Then run a mile segment at 8:48, and run a second mile with a total time of 17:36, and continue at the same pace per mile for 1-2 more miles. From the beginning of these segments, take a 50 second walk break after 4 minutes of running. This means that you will have to pick up the pace by a few seconds per minute to maintain your 8:48 pace by the watch. Stay smooth and try to maintain the same pace. This trains you to run at race pace, taking walk breaks.

12. It is fine to do cross training on Monday and Friday, if you wish. Except for running in the water, cross training doesn't tend to improve performance. Avoid exercises like stair machines (during rest days from running) that use the calf muscles.

13. Be sure to take a vacation from strenuous exercise the day before your long runs and mile repetitions.

14. On Friday, run a few hill repeats (h), as described in the hill section in this book. The Acg's will get the legs warmed up for the hill accelerations. The length of the hills should be 200 meters to 300 meters. Walk down most of each hill for almost complete recovery.

15. Hills (h) are suggested on short mileage weekends, during the early weeks of the program. Start with 2 hill repeats and increase by one hill on each successive workout until you reach 5 hills, as noted on the schedule. Because Boston has some significant hills in strategic locations, these workouts are crucial. The hills are embedded into the total mileage for the day.

16. Double workouts can be run on Tuesday and Friday. See the chapter in this book called "For Extra Credit."

17. During the last two weeks of the program, you cannot improve performance so avoid running too fast. On some of the short mile days, however, it is OK to run a 2 mile segment running 8:48 pace, while taking a 50 second walk break after each 4 minutes of running. This fine-tunes your pace judgment and your mental focus.

18. Never run through pain—read the chapter on injuries if you sense that you have the beginning of an injury.

Mon	Tue (CDAcg/p)	Wed	Thurs (CD)	Fri (Acg/h)	Sat	Sun
Week 1						
off	45 min run	off or XT	30 min run	40 min	off	7 miles
Week 2						
off	45 min run	off/XT	30 min run	40 min	off	8 miles
Week 3						
off	50 min run	off/XT	30 min run	40 min	off	5 mi with 2 hills
Week 4						
off	50 min run	off/XT	30 min run	40 min	off	9.5 miles
Week 5						
off	40 min run	off/XT	30 min run	45 min	off	5 mi with 3 hills
Week 6						
off	50 min run	off/XT	30 min run	45 min	off	11 miles
Week 7						
off	40 min run	off/XT	30 min run	45 min	off	6 mi with 4 hills
Week 8						
off	55 min run	off/XT	30 min run	45 min	off	13 miles
Week 9						
off	40 min run	off/XT	30 min run	50 min	off	6 mi with 5 hills
Week 10						
off	55 min run	off/XT	30 min run	50 min	off	15 miles
Week 11						
off	40 min run	off/XT	30 min run	50 min	off	2 x 2 mile
Week 12						
off	60 min run	off/XT	30 min run	50 min	off	17 miles
Week 13						
off	40 min run	off/XT	30 min run	60 min	off	3 x 2 mile
Week 14						
off	60 min run	off/XT	30 min run	60 min	off	8 miles MM
Week 15						
off	65 min run	off/XT	30 min run	60 min	off	20 miles

Week 16						
off	45 min run	off/XT	30 min run	50 min	off	4 x 2 mile

Week 17						
off	65 min run	off/XT	30 min run	65 min	off	7 miles MM

Week 18						
off	65 min run	off/XT	30 min run	60 min	off	23 miles

Week 19						
off	45 min run	off/XT	30 min run	60 min	off	5 x 2 mile

Week 20						
off	60 min run	off/XT	30 min run	65 min	off	7 miles MM

Week 21						
off	60 min run	off/XT	30 min run	60 min	off	26 miles

Week 22						
off	45 min run	off/XT	30 min run	65 min	off	6 miles

Week 23						
off	60 min run	off/XT	30 min run	60 min	off	6 x 2 mile

Week 24						
off	60 min run	off/XT	30 min run	65 min	off	7 miles MM

Week 25						
off	60 min run	off/XT	30 min run	60 min	off	29 miles

Week 26						
off	60 min run	off/XT	30 min run	65 min	off	6 miles

Week 27						
off	60 min run	off/XT	30 min run	60 min	off	7 x 2 miles

Week 28						
off	45 min run	off/XT	30 min run	60 min	off	Goal Race/Boston

Week 30 (Recovery week)						
off/XT	40 min run	off/XT	30 min run	30 min	off	off

Time goal 4:00

Note: This is the minimum that I've found necessary to prepare for the goal. If you are already running more than this amount, and are able to recover between workouts, you may continue to do what you are doing—but be careful.

1. To begin this program, you should have run a long run within the past 2 weeks of at least 6 miles. If your long run is not this long, then gradually increase the weekend run to this distance before starting the program.

2. If your current long run is longer than 7 miles, it is possible to start on the week with a long run that is at or slightly longer than the distance of the longest run you have run in the past 2 weeks. For example, if you ran 13 miles two weeks ago, you could start with week # 8, # 9 or # 10. In this case, you will lose the benefits from the hill workouts on the short mileage weekends.

3. What is your current level of performance? The "magic mile" time trials, noted by MM on the schedule, will tell you. Read the chapter in this book on "Choosing the Right Goal..." Take your current MM and multiply by 1.3. This predicts your best possible per mile performance in the marathon under ideal conditions when you've done all of the training. Follow the instructions in that chapter to set a realistic goal and to monitor your progress. The MM is run once on each weekend noted in the schedule. You can run any pace you wish for the remaining miles assigned on these workouts. To predict a 4:00 marathon performance, your MM should be 6:58 or faster by the end of the program.

4. What pace should I run on the long runs? Take your current performance level (MM x 1.3) and add 2 minutes. The result is your suggested long run pace per mile on long runs at 60F or cooler. For those who are currently predicting a 4:00 in the marathon, the long run pace should be no faster than 11:10/mile at 60F and 12:10/mi at 70F. It is always better to run slower to ensure faster recovery.

5. On long runs, and in the marathon itself, slow down even more when the temperature rises: by 30 seconds a mile for every 5 degrees above 60F.

6. Run-Walk-Run ratio should correspond to the pace used (See the Run-Walk-Run chapter in this book).

7. Most runners don't improve more than 30 seconds per mile during a 30-week marathon training program. If your goal is more aggressive, you may increase injury stress during the training or may be frustrated with your final time. Use the MMs as reality checks on your current performance level, and remember that they are based upon "ideal projections."

8. Speed repetitions of 2 miles each are listed on the schedule for this goal. During each 2 miler, run the first and the last 800 meters in 4:25, and run the mile in the middle in 8:30. After each 800 meter, walk for 30 seconds. Stay smooth. If you are struggling to maintain pace, slow down to run efficiently. If you are slowing down significantly during the second mile, shift to running twice as many 1 mile repeats. Be sure to read the section in this book on speed training.

9. Warm up for each 2 mile repeat workout by walking for 2-5 minutes, then jog very slowly for 5-10 minutes. Next, do 4-8 acceleration-gliders (see the segment about this in this book). Reverse this process as you warm down, leaving out the acceleration gliders.

10. Recover between each 2 mile repeat by walking and jogging for 7 minutes between each. You may choose the amount of walking vs. jogging. If you are using a heart monitor, your heart rate should drop below 65 % of max heart rate before starting another 2 mile repeat.

11. If you have recovered from the weekend run, during your Tuesday workout run 2-4 miles at race pace (noted as "p" on the Tue line). After an easy warm-up, run 4 of the acceleration-gliders (Acg). (These are described in the drill section of this book). Then run a mile segment at 9:00, walk for one minute, and run a second mile with a total time of 18:00, and continue at the same pace per mile for 1-2 more miles. From the beginning of these segments, take a 1 minute walk break after 4 minutes of running. This means that you will have to pick up the pace by a few seconds per minute to maintain your 9:00 pace by the watch. Stay smooth and try to maintain the same pace. This trains you to run at race pace, taking walk breaks.

12. It is fine to do cross training on Monday and Friday, if you wish. Except for running in the water, cross training doesn't tend to improve performance. Avoid exercises like stair machines (during rest days from running) that use the calf muscles.

13. Be sure to take a vacation from strenuous exercise the day before your long runs and mile repetitions.

14. On Friday, run a few hill repeats (h), as described in the hill section in this book. The Acg's will get the legs warmed up for the hill accelerations. The length of the hills should be 200 meters to 300 meters. Walk down most of each hill for almost complete recovery.

15. Hills (h) are suggested on short mileage weekends, during the early weeks of the program. Start with 2 hill repeats and increase by one hill on each successive workout until you reach 5 hills, as noted on the schedule. Because Boston has some significant hills in strategic locations, these workouts are crucial. The hills are embedded into the total mileage for the day.

16. Double workouts can be run on Tuesday and Friday. See the chapter in this book called "For Extra Credit."

17. During the last two weeks of the program, you cannot improve performance so avoid running too fast. On some of the short mile days, however, it is OK to run a 2 mile segment running 9:00 pace, while taking a 1 minute walk break after each 4 minutes of running. This fine-tunes your pace judgment and your mental focus.

18. Never run through pain—read the chapter on injuries if you sense that you have the beginning of an injury.

Mon	Tue (CDAcg/p)	Wed	Thurs (CD)	Fri (Acg/h)	Sat	Sun
Week 1						
off	45 min run	off or XT	30 min run	40 min	off	7 miles
Week 2						
off	45 min run	off/XT	30 min run	40 min	off	8 miles
Week 3						
off	50 min run	off/XT	30 min run	40 min	off	5 mi with 2 hills
Week 4						
off	50 min run	off/XT	30 min run	40 min	off	9.5 miles
Week 5						
off	40 min run	off/XT	30 min run	45 min	off	5 mi with 3 hills
Week 6						
off	50 min run	off/XT	30 min run	45 min	off	11 miles
Week 7						
off	40 min run	off/XT	30 min run	45 min	off	6 mi with 4 hills
Week 8						
off	55 min run	off/XT	30 min run	45 min	off	13 miles
Week 9						
off	40 min run	off/XT	30 min run	50 min	off	6 mi with 5 hills
Week 10						
off	55 min run	off/XT	30 min run	50 min	off	15 miles
Week 11						
off	40 min run	off/XT	30 min run	50 min	off	2 x 2 mile
Week 12						
off	60 min run	off/XT	30 min run	50 min	off	17 miles
Week 13						
off	40 min run	off/XT	30 min run	60 min	off	3 x 2 mile
Week 14						
off	60 min run	off/XT	30 min run	60 min	off	8 miles MM
Week 15						
off	65 min run	off/XT	30 min run	60 min	off	20 miles

Week 16						
off	45 min run	off/XT	30 min run	50 min	off	4 x 2 mile

Week 17						
off	65 min run	off/XT	30 min run	65 min	off	7 miles MM

Week 18						
off	65 min run	off/XT	30 min run	60 min	off	23 miles

Week 19						
off	45 min run	off/XT	30 min run	60 min	off	5 x 2 mile

Week 20						
off	60 min run	off/XT	30 min run	65 min	off	7 miles MM

Week 21						
off	60 min run	off/XT	30 min run	60 min	off	26 miles

Week 22						
off	45 min run	off/XT	30 min run	65 min	off	6 miles

Week 23						
off	60 min run	off/XT	30 min run	60 min	off	6 x 2 mile

Week 24						
off	60 min run	off/XT	30 min run	65 min	off	7 miles MM

Week 25						
off	60 min run	off/XT	30 min run	60 min	off	29 miles

Week 26						
off	60 min run	off/XT	30 min run	65 min	off	6 miles

Week 27						
off	60 min run	off/XT	30 min run	60 min	off	7 x 2 miles

Week 28						
off	45 min run	off/XT	30 min run	60 min	off	7 miles

Week 29						
off	40 min run	off/XT	30 min run	30 min	off	Goal Race/Boston

Week 30 (Recovery week)						
off/XT	30 min run	off/XT	30 min run	off	5 miles	off

Time goal 4:10

Note: This is the minimum that I've found necessary to prepare for the goal. If you are already running more than this amount, and are able to recover between workouts, you may continue to do what you are doing—but be careful.

1. To begin this program, you should have run a long run within the past 2 weeks of at least 6 miles. If your long run is not this long, then gradually increase the weekend run to this distance before starting the program.
2. If your current long run is longer than 7 miles, it is possible to start on the week with a long run that is at or slightly longer than the distance of the longest run you have run in the past 2 weeks. For example, if you ran 13 miles two weeks ago, you could start with week # 8, # 9 or # 10. In this case, you will lose the benefits from the hill workouts on the short mileage weekends.
3. What is your current level of performance? The "magic mile" time trials, noted by MM on the schedule, will tell you. Read the chapter in this book on "Choosing the Right Goal..." Take your current MM and multiply by 1.3. This predicts your best possible per mile performance in the marathon under ideal conditions when you've done all of the training. Follow the instructions in that chapter to set a realistic goal and to monitor your progress. The MM is run once on each weekend noted in the schedule. You can run any pace you wish for the remaining miles assigned on these workouts. To predict a 4:10 marathon performance, your MM should be 7:15 or faster by the end of the program.
4. What pace should I run on the long runs? Take your current performance level (MM x 1.3) and add 2 minutes. The result is your suggested long run pace per mile on long runs at 60F or cooler. For those who are currently predicting a 4:10 in the marathon, the long run pace should be no faster than 11:30/mile at 60F and 12:30/mi at 70F. It is always better to run slower to ensure faster recovery.
5. On long runs, and in the marathon itself, slow down even more when the temperature rises: by 30 seconds a mile for every 5 degrees above 60F.
6. Run-Walk-Run ratio should correspond to the pace used (See the Run-Walk-Run chapter in this book).
7. Most runners don't improve more than 30 seconds per mile during a 30-week marathon training program. If your goal is more aggressive, you may increase injury stress during the training or may be frustrated with your final time. Use the MMs as reality checks on your current performance level, and remember that they are based upon "ideal projections."
8. Speed repetitions of 1 mile each are listed on the schedule for this goal. During each mile repeat, take a 30 second walk break after 3 minutes of running. Run the first and the last mile repeat in 9:10, and the others in 8:40. Stay smooth. If you are struggling to maintain pace, slow down to run efficiently. If you are slowing down significantly during the second half, shift to running twice as many 800 meter repeats. Be sure to read the section in this book on speed training.

9. Warm up for each mile repeat workout by walking for 2-5 minutes, then jog very slowly for 5-10 minutes. Next, do 4-8 acceleration-gliders (see the segment about this in this book). Reverse this process as you warm down, leaving out the acceleration gliders.

10. Recover between each mile repeat by walking and jogging for 5 minutes between each. You may choose the amount of walking vs. jogging. If you are using a heart monitor, your heart rate should drop below 65 % of max heart rate before starting another mile repeat.

11. If you have recovered from the weekend run, during your Tuesday workout run 2-4 miles at race pace (noted as "p" on the Tue line). After an easy warm-up, run 4 of the acceleration-gliders (Acg). (These are described in the drill section of this book). Then run a mile segment at 9:20, and run a second mile with a total time of 18:40, and continue at the same pace per mile for 1-2 more miles. From the beginning of these segments, take a 1 minute walk break after 3 minutes of running. This means that you will have to pick up the pace by a few seconds per minute to maintain your 9:20 pace by the watch. Stay smooth and try to maintain the same pace. This trains you to run at race pace, taking walk breaks.

12. It is fine to do cross training on Monday and Friday, if you wish. Except for running in the water, cross training doesn't tend to improve performance. Avoid exercises like stair machines (during rest days from running) that use the calf muscles.

13. Be sure to take a vacation from strenuous exercise the day before your long runs and mile repetitions.

14. On Friday, run a few hill repeats (h), as described in the hill section in this book. The Acg's will get the legs warmed up for the hill accelerations. The length of the hills should be 200 meters to 250 meters. Walk down most of each hill for almost complete recovery.

15. Hills (h) are suggested on short mileage weekends, during the early weeks of the program. Start with 2 hill repeats and increase by one hill on each successive workout until you reach 5 hills, as noted on the schedule. Because Boston has some significant hills in strategic locations, these workouts are crucial. The hills are embedded into the total mileage for the day.

16. Double workouts can be run on Tuesday and Friday. See the chapter in this book called "For Extra Credit."

17. During the last two weeks of the program, you cannot improve performance so avoid running too fast. On some of the short mile days, however, it is OK to run a 2-3 mile segment running 9:20 pace, while taking a 1 minute walk break after each 3 minutes of running. This fine-tunes your pace judgment and your mental focus.

18. Never run through pain—read the chapter on injuries if you sense that you have the beginning of an injury.

Mon	Tue (CDAcg/p)	Wed	Thurs (CD)	Fri (Acg/h)	Sat	Sun
Week 1						
off	45 min run	off or XT	30 min run	40 min	off	7 miles
Week 2						
off	45 min run	off/XT	30 min run	40 min	off	8 miles
Week 3						
off	50 min run	off/XT	30 min run	40 min	off	5 mi with 2 hills
Week 4						
off	50 min run	off/XT	30 min run	40 min	off	9.5 miles
Week 5						
off	40 min run	off/XT	30 min run	45 min	off	5 mi with 3 hills
Week 6						
off	50 min run	off/XT	30 min run	45 min	off	11 miles
Week 7						
off	40 min run	off/XT	30 min run	45 min	off	6 mi with 4 hills
Week 8						
off	55 min run	off/XT	30 min run	45 min	off	13 miles
Week 9						
off	40 min run	off/XT	30 min run	50 min	off	6 mi with 5 hills
Week 10						
off	55 min run	off/XT	30 min run	50 min	off	15 miles
Week 11						
off	40 min run	off/XT	30 min run	50 min	off	4 x 1 mile
Week 12						
off	60 min run	off/XT	30 min run	50 min	off	17 miles
Week 13						
off	40 min run	off/XT	30 min run	60 min	off	6 x 1 mile
Week 14						
off	60 min run	off/XT	30 min run	60 min	off	8 miles MM
Week 15						
off	65 min run	off/XT	30 min run	60 min	off	20 miles

Week 16						
off	45 min run	off/XT	30 min run	50 min	off	10 x 1 mile
Week 17						
off	65 min run	off/XT	30 min run	65 min	off	7 miles MM
Week 18						
off	65 min run	off/XT	30 min run	60 min	off	23 miles
Week 19						
off	45 min run	off/XT	30 min run	60 min	off	10 x 1 mile
Week 20						
off	60 min run	off/XT	30 min run	65 min	off	7 miles MM
Week 21						
off	60 min run	off/XT	30 min run	60 min	off	26 miles
Week 22						
off	45 min run	off/XT	30 min run	65 min	off	6 miles
Week 23						
off	60 min run	off/XT	30 min run	60 min	off	12 x 1 mile
Week 24						
off	60 min run	off/XT	30 min run	65 min	off	7 miles MM
Week 25						
off	60 min run	off/XT	30 min run	60 min	off	29 miles
Week 26						
off	60 min run	off/XT	30 min run	65 min	off	6 miles
Week 27						
off	60 min run	off/XT	30 min run	60 min	off	14 x 1 mile
Week 28						
off	45 min run	off/XT	30 min run	60 min	off	7 miles
Week 29						
off	40 min run	off/XT	30 min run	30 min	off	Goal Race/Boston
Week 30 (Recovery week)						
off/XT	30 min run	off/XT	30 min run	off	5 miles	off

Time goal 4:25

Note: This is the minimum that I've found necessary to prepare for the goal. If you are already running more than this amount, and are able to recover between workouts, you may continue to do what you are doing—but be careful.

1. To begin this program, you should have run a long run within the past 2 weeks of at least 6 miles. If your long run is not this long, then gradually increase the weekend run to this distance before starting the program.
2. If your current long run is longer than 7 miles, it is possible to start on the week with a long run that is at or slightly longer than the distance of the longest run you have run in the past 2 weeks. For example, if you ran 13 miles two weeks ago, you could start with week # 8, # 9 or # 10. In this case, you will lose the benefits from the hill workouts on the short mileage weekends.
3. What is your current level of performance? The "magic mile" time trials, noted by MM on the schedule, will tell you. Read the chapter in this book on "Choosing the Right Goal..." Take your current MM and multiply by 1.3. This predicts your best possible per mile performance in the marathon under ideal conditions when you've done all of the training. Follow the instructions in that chapter to set a realistic goal and to monitor your progress. The MM is run once on each weekend noted in the schedule. You can run any pace you wish for the remaining miles assigned on these workouts. To predict a 4:25 marathon performance, your MM should be 7:35 or faster by the end of the program.
4. What pace should I run on the long runs? Take your current performance level (MM x 1.3) and add 2 minutes. The result is your suggested long run pace per mile on long runs at 60F or cooler. For those who are currently predicting a 4:25 in the marathon, the long run pace should be no faster than 12:00/mile at 60F and 13:00/mi at 70F. It is always better to run slower to ensure faster recovery.
5. On long runs, and in the marathon itself, slow down even more when the temperature rises: by 30 seconds a mile for every 5 degrees above 60F.
6. Run-Walk-Run ratio should correspond to the pace used (See the Run-Walk-Run chapter in this book).
7. Most runners don't improve more than 30 seconds per mile during a 30-week marathon training program. If your goal is more aggressive, you may increase injury stress during the training or may be frustrated with your final time. Use the MMs as reality checks on your current performance level, and remember that they are based upon "ideal projections."
8. Speed repetitions of 1 mile each are listed on the schedule for this goal. During each mile repeat, take a 30 second walk break after 3 minutes of running. Run the first and the last mile repeat in 9:30, and the others in 9:10. Stay smooth. If you are struggling to maintain pace, slow down to run efficiently. If you are slowing down significantly during the second half, shift to running twice as many 800 meter repeats. Be sure to read the section in this book on speed training.

9. Warm up for each mile repeat workout by walking for 2-5 minutes, then jog very slowly for 5-10 minutes. Next, do 4-8 acceleration-gliders (see the segment about this in this book). Reverse this process as you warm down, leaving out the acceleration gliders.

10. Recover between each mile repeat by walking and jogging for 5 minutes between each. You may choose the amount of walking vs. jogging. If you are using a heart monitor, your heart rate should drop below 65 % of max heart rate before starting another mile repeat.

11. If you have recovered from the weekend run, during your Tuesday workout run 2-4 miles at race pace (noted as "p" on the Tue line). After an easy warm-up, run 4 of the acceleration-gliders (Acg). (These are described in the drill section of this book). Then run a mile segment at 9:42, and run a second mile with a total time of 19:24, and continue at the same pace per mile for 1-2 more miles. From the beginning of these segments, take a 1 minute walk break after 3 minutes of running. This means that you will have to pick up the pace by a few seconds per minute to maintain your 9:42 pace by the watch. Stay smooth and try to maintain the same pace. This trains you to run at race pace, taking walk breaks.

12. It is fine to do cross training on Monday and Friday, if you wish. Except for running in the water, cross training doesn't tend to improve performance. Avoid exercises like stair machines (during rest days from running) that use the calf muscles.

13. Be sure to take a vacation from strenuous exercise the day before your long runs and mile repetitions.

14. On Friday, run a few hill repeats (h), as described in the hill section in this book. The Acg's will get the legs warmed up for the hill accelerations. The length of the hills should be 200 meters to 300 meters. Walk down most of each hill for almost complete recovery.

15. Hills (h) are suggested on short mileage weekends, during the early weeks of the program. Start with 2 hill repeats and increase by one hill on each successive workout until you reach 5 hills, as noted on the schedule. Because Boston has some significant hills in strategic locations, these workouts are crucial. The hills are embedded into the total mileage for the day.

16. Double workouts can be run on Tuesday and Friday. See the chapter in this book called "For Extra Credit."

17. During the last two weeks of the program, you cannot improve performance so avoid running too fast. On some of the short mile days, however, it is OK to run a 2 mile segment running 9:42 pace, while taking a 1 minute walk break after running for 3 minutes. This fine-tunes your pace judgment and your mental focus.

18. Never run through pain—read the chapter on injuries if you sense that you have the beginning of an injury.

Mon	Tue (CDAcg/p)	Wed	Thurs (CD)	Fri (Acg/h)	Sat	Sun
Week 1						
off	45 min run	off or XT	30 min run	40 min	off	7 miles
Week 2						
off	45 min run	off/XT	30 min run	40 min	off	8 miles
Week 3						
off	50 min run	off/XT	30 min run	40 min	off	5 mi with 2 hills
Week 4						
off	50 min run	off/XT	30 min run	40 min	off	9.5 miles
Week 5						
off	40 min run	off/XT	30 min run	45 min	off	5 mi with 3 hills
Week 6						
off	50 min run	off/XT	30 min run	45 min	off	11 miles
Week 7						
off	40 min run	off/XT	30 min run	45 min	off	6 mi with 4 hills
Week 8						
off	55 min run	off/XT	30 min run	45 min	off	13 miles
Week 9						
off	40 min run	off/XT	30 min run	50 min	off	6 mi with 5 hills
Week 10						
off	55 min run	off/XT	30 min run	50 min	off	15 miles
Week 11						
off	40 min run	off/XT	30 min run	50 min	off	4 x 1 mile
Week 12						
off	60 min run	off/XT	30 min run	50 min	off	17 miles
Week 13						
off	40 min run	off/XT	30 min run	60 min	off	6 x 1 mile
Week 14						
off	60 min run	off/XT	30 min run	60 min	off	8 miles MM
Week 15						
off	65 min run	off/XT	30 min run	60 min	off	20 miles

Week 16						
off	45 min run	off/XT	30 min run	50 min	off	10 x 1 mile

Week 17						
off	65 min run	off/XT	30 min run	65 min	off	7 miles MM

Week 18						
off	65 min run	off/XT	30 min run	60 min	off	23 miles

Week 19						
off	45 min run	off/XT	30 min run	60 min	off	10 x 1 mile

Week 20						
off	60 min run	off/XT	30 min run	65 min	off	7 miles MM

Week 21						
off	60 min run	off/XT	30 min run	60 min	off	26 miles

Week 22						
off	45 min run	off/XT	30 min run	65 min	off	6 miles

Week 23						
off	60 min run	off/XT	30 min run	60 min	off	12 x 1 mile

Week 24						
off	60 min run	off/XT	30 min run	65 min	off	7 miles MM

Week 25						
off	60 min run	off/XT	30 min run	60 min	off	29 miles

Week 26						
off	60 min run	off/XT	30 min run	65 min	off	6 miles

Week 27						
off	60 min run	off/XT	30 min run	60 min	off	14 x 1 mile

Week 28						
off	45 min run	off/XT	30 min run	60 min	off	7 miles

Week 29						
off	40 min run	off/XT	30 min run	30 min	off	Goal Race/Boston

Week 30 (Recovery week)						
off/XT	30 min run	off/XT	30 min run	off	5 miles	off

Time goal 4:40

Note: This is the minimum that I've found necessary to prepare for the goal. If you are already running more than this amount, and are able to recover between workouts, you may continue to do what you are doing—but be careful.

1. To begin this program, you should have run a long run within the past 2 weeks of at least 6 miles. If your long run is not this long, then gradually increase the weekend run to this distance before starting the program.

2. If your current long run is longer than 7 miles, it is possible to start on the week with a long run that is at or slightly longer than the distance of the longest run you have run in the past 2 weeks. For example, if you ran 13 miles two weeks ago, you could start with week # 8, # 9 or # 10. In this case, you will lose the benefits from the hill workouts on the short mileage weekends.

3. What is your current level of performance? The "magic mile" time trials, noted by MM on the schedule, will tell you. Read the chapter in this book on "Choosing the Right Goal..." Take your current MM and multiply by 1.3. This predicts your best possible per mile performance in the marathon under ideal conditions when you've done all of the training. Follow the instructions in that chapter to set a realistic goal and to monitor your progress. The MM is run once on each weekend noted in the schedule. You can run any pace you wish for the remaining miles assigned on these workouts. To predict a 4:40 marathon performance, your MM should be 8:05 or faster by the end of the program.

4. What pace should I run on the long runs? Take your current performance level (MM x 1.3) and add 2 minutes. The result is your suggested long run pace per mile on long runs at 60F or cooler. For those who are currently predicting a 4:40 in the marathon, the long run pace should be no faster than 12:30/mile at 60F and 13:30/mi at 70F. It is always better to run slower to ensure faster recovery.

5. On long runs, and in the marathon itself, slow down even more when the temperature rises: by 30 seconds a mile for every 5 degrees above 60F.

6. Run-Walk-Run ratio should correspond to the pace used (See the Run-Walk-Run chapter in this book).

7. Most runners don't improve more than 30 seconds per mile during a 30-week marathon training program. If your goal is more aggressive, you may increase injury stress during the training or may be frustrated with your final time. Use the MMs as reality checks on your current performance level, and remember that they are based upon "ideal projections."

8. Speed repetitions of 1 mile each are listed on the schedule for this goal. During each mile repeat, take a 30 second walk break after 3 minutes of running. Run the first and the last mile repeat in 10:05, and the others in 9:45. Stay smooth. If you are struggling to maintain pace, slow down to run efficiently. If you are slowing down significantly during the second half, shift to running twice as many 800 meter repeats. Be sure to read the section in this book on speed training.

9. Warm up for each mile repeat workout by walking for 2-5 minutes, then jog very slowly for 5-10 minutes. Next, do 4-8 acceleration-gliders (see the segment about this in this book). Reverse this process as you warm down, leaving out the acceleration gliders.

10. Recover between each mile repeat by walking and jogging for 5 minutes between each. You may choose the amount of walking vs. jogging. If you are using a heart monitor, your heart rate should drop below 65 % of max heart rate before starting another mile repeat.

11. If you have recovered from the weekend run, during your Tuesday workout run 2-4 miles at race pace (noted as "p" on the Tue line). After an easy warm-up, run 4 of the acceleration-gliders (Acg). (These are described in the drill section of this book). Then run a mile segment at 10:15, and run a second mile with a total time of 20:30, and continue at the same pace per mile for 1-2 more miles. From the beginning of these segments, take a 1 minute walk break after 3 minutes of running. This means that you will have to pick up the pace by a few seconds per minute to maintain your 10:15 pace by the watch. Stay smooth and try to maintain the same pace. This trains you to run at race pace, taking walk breaks.

12. It is fine to do cross training on Monday and Friday, if you wish. Except for running in the water, cross training doesn't tend to improve performance. Avoid exercises like stair machines (during rest days from running) that use the calf muscles.

13. Be sure to take a vacation from strenuous exercise the day before your long runs and mile repetitions.

14. On Friday, run a few hill repeats (h), as described in the hill section in this book. The Acg's will get the legs warmed up for the hill accelerations. The length of the hills should be 200 meters to 250 meters. Walk down most of each hill for almost complete recovery.

15. Hills (h) are suggested on short mileage weekends, during the early weeks of the program. Start with 2 hill repeats and increase by one hill on each successive workout until you reach 5 hills, as noted on the schedule. Because Boston has some significant hills in strategic locations, these workouts are crucial. The hills are embedded into the total mileage for the day.

16. Double workouts can be run on Tuesday and Friday. See the chapter in this book called "For Extra Credit."

17. During the last two weeks of the program, you cannot improve performance so avoid running too fast. On some of the short mile days, however, it is OK to run a 2 mile segment running 10:15 pace, while taking a 1 minute walk break after each 3 minutes of running. This fine-tunes your pace judgment and your mental focus.

18. Never run through pain—read the chapter on injuries if you sense that you have the beginning of an injury.

Mon	Tue (CDAcg/p)	Wed	Thurs (CD)	Fri (Acg/h)	Sat	Sun
Week 1						
off	45 min run	off or XT	30 min run	40 min	off	7 miles
Week 2						
off	45 min run	off/XT	30 min run	40 min	off	8 miles
Week 3						
off	50 min run	off/XT	30 min run	40 min	off	5 mi with 2 hills
Week 4						
off	50 min run	off/XT	30 min run	40 min	off	9.5 miles
Week 5						
off	40 min run	off/XT	30 min run	45 min	off	5 mi with 3 hills
Week 6						
off	50 min run	off/XT	30 min run	45 min	off	11 miles
Week 7						
off	40 min run	off/XT	30 min run	45 min	off	6 mi with 4 hills
Week 8						
off	55 min run	off/XT	30 min run	45 min	off	13 miles
Week 9						
off	40 min run	off/XT	30 min run	50 min	off	6 mi with 5 hills
Week 10						
off	55 min run	off/XT	30 min run	50 min	off	15 miles
Week 11						
off	40 min run	off/XT	30 min run	50 min	off	4 x 1 mile
Week 12						
off	60 min run	off/XT	30 min run	50 min	off	17 miles
Week 13						
off	40 min run	off/XT	30 min run	60 min	off	6 x 1 mile
Week 14						
off	60 min run	off/XT	30 min run	60 min	off	8 miles MM
Week 15						
off	65 min run	off/XT	30 min run	60 min	off	20 miles

Week 16						
off	45 min run	off/XT	30 min run	50 min	off	10 x 1 mile

Week 17						
off	65 min run	off/XT	30 min run	65 min	off	7 miles MM

Week 18						
off	65 min run	off/XT	30 min run	60 min	off	23 miles

Week 19						
off	45 min run	off/XT	30 min run	60 min	off	10 x 1 mile

Week 20						
off	60 min run	off/XT	30 min run	65 min	off	7 miles MM

Week 21						
off	60 min run	off/XT	30 min run	60 min	off	26 miles

Week 22						
off	45 min run	off/XT	30 min run	65 min	off	6 miles

Week 23						
off	60 min run	off/XT	30 min run	60 min	off	12 x 1 mile

Week 24						
off	60 min run	off/XT	30 min run	65 min	off	7 miles MM

Week 25						
off	60 min run	off/XT	30 min run	60 min	off	29 miles

Week 26						
off	60 min run	off/XT	30 min run	65 min	off	6 miles

Week 27						
off	60 min run	off/XT	30 min run	60 min	off	14 x 1 mile

Week 28						
off	45 min run	off/XT	30 min run	60 min	off	7 miles

Week 29						
off	40 min run	off/XT	30 min run	30 min	off	Goal Race/Boston

Week 30 (Recovery week)						
off/XT	30 min run	off/XT	30 min run	off	5 miles	off

Time goal 4:55

Note: This is the minimum that I've found necessary to prepare for the goal. If you are already running more than this amount, and are able to recover between workouts, you may continue to do what you are doing—but be careful.

1. To begin this program, you should have run a long run within the past 2 weeks of at least 6 miles. If your long run is not this long, then gradually increase the weekend run to this distance before starting the program.

2. If your current long run is longer than 7 miles, it is possible to start on the week with a long run that is at or slightly longer than the distance of the longest run you have run in the past 2 weeks. For example, if you ran 13 miles two weeks ago, you could start with week # 8, # 9 or # 10. In this case, you will lose the benefits from the hill workouts on the short mileage weekends.

3. What is your current level of performance? The "magic mile" time trials, noted by MM on the schedule, will tell you. Read the chapter in this book on "Choosing the Right Goal..." Take your current MM and multiply by 1.3. This predicts your best possible per mile performance in the marathon under ideal conditions when you've done all of the training. Follow the instructions in that chapter to set a realistic goal and to monitor your progress. The MM is run once on each weekend noted in the schedule. You can run any pace you wish for the remaining miles assigned on these workouts. To predict a 4:55 marathon performance, your MM should be 8:40 or faster by the end of the program.

4. What pace should I run on the long runs? Take your current performance level (MM x 1.3) and add 2 minutes. The result is your suggested long run pace per mile on long runs at 60F or cooler. For those who are currently predicting a 4:55 in the marathon, the long run pace should be no faster than 13:30/mile at 60F and 14:30/mi at 70F. It is always better to run slower to ensure faster recovery.

5. On long runs, and in the marathon itself, slow down even more when the temperature rises: by 30 seconds a mile for every 5 degrees above 60F.

6. Run-Walk-Run ratio should correspond to the pace used (See the Run-Walk-Run chapter in this book).

7. Most runners don't improve more than 30 seconds per mile during a 30-week marathon training program. If your goal is more aggressive, you may increase injury stress during the training or may be frustrated with your final time. Use the MMs as reality checks on your current performance level, and remember that they are based upon "ideal projections."

8. Speed repetitions of 1 mile each are listed on the schedule for this goal. During each mile repeat, take a 30 second walk break after running for 2:30. Run the first and the last mile repeat in 11:15, and the others in 10:50. Stay smooth. If you are struggling to maintain pace, slow down to run efficiently. If you are slowing down significantly during the second half, shift to running twice as many 800 meter repeats. Be sure to read the section in this book on speed training.

9. Warm up for each mile repeat workout by walking for 2-5 minutes, then jog very slowly for 5-10 minutes. Next, do 4-8 acceleration-gliders (see the segment about this in this book). Reverse this process as you warm down, leaving out the acceleration gliders.

10. Recover between each mile repeat by walking and jogging for 5 minutes between each. You may choose the amount of walking vs. jogging. If you are using a heart monitor, your heart rate should drop below 65 % of max heart rate before starting another mile repeat.

11. If you have recovered from the weekend run, during your Tuesday workout run 2-4 miles at race pace (noted as "p" on the Tue line). After an easy warm-up, run 4 of the acceleration-gliders (Acg). (These are described in the drill section of this book). Then run a mile segment at 11:25, and run a second mile with a total time of 22:50, and continue at the same pace per mile for 1-2 more miles. From the beginning of these segments, take a 1 minute walk break after running for 2:30. This means that you will have to pick up the pace by a few seconds per minute to maintain your 11:30 pace by the watch. Stay smooth and try to maintain the same pace. This trains you to run at race pace, taking walk breaks.

12. It is fine to do cross training on Monday and Friday, if you wish. Except for running in the water, cross training doesn't tend to improve performance. Avoid exercises like stair machines (during rest days from running) that use the calf muscles.

13. Be sure to take a vacation from strenuous exercise the day before your long runs and mile repetitions.

14. On Friday, run a few hill repeats (h), as described in the hill section in this book. The Acg's will get the legs warmed up for the hill accelerations. The length of the hills should be 200 meters to 250 meters. Walk down most of each hill for almost complete recovery.

15. Hills (h) are suggested on short mileage weekends, during the early weeks of the program. Start with 2 hill repeats and increase by one hill on each successive workout until you reach 5 hills, as noted on the schedule. Because Boston has some significant hills in strategic locations, these workouts are crucial. The hills are embedded into the total mileage for the day.

16. Double workouts can be run on Tuesday and Friday. See the chapter in this book called "For Extra Credit."

17. During the last two weeks of the program, you cannot improve performance so avoid running too fast. On some of the short mile days, however, it is OK to run a 2 mile segment running 11:25 pace, while taking a 1 minute walk break after running for 2:30. This fine-tunes your pace judgment and your mental focus.

18. Never run through pain—read the chapter on injuries if you sense that you have the beginning of an injury.

Mon	Tue (CDAcg/p)	Wed	Thurs (CD)	Fri (Acg/h)	Sat	Sun
Week 1						
off	45 min run	off or XT	30 min run	40 min	off	7 miles
Week 2						
off	45 min run	off/XT	30 min run	40 min	off	8 miles
Week 3						
off	50 min run	off/XT	30 min run	40 min	off	5 mi with 2 hills
Week 4						
off	50 min run	off/XT	30 min run	40 min	off	9.5 miles
Week 5						
off	40 min run	off/XT	30 min run	45 min	off	5 mi with 3 hills
Week 6						
off	50 min run	off/XT	30 min run	45 min	off	11 miles
Week 7						
off	40 min run	off/XT 3	0 min run	45 min	off	6 mi with 4 hills
Week 8						
off	55 min run	off/XT	30 min run	45 min	off	13 miles
Week 9						
off	40 min run	off/XT	30 min run	50 min	off	6 mi with 5 hills
Week 10						
off	55 min run	off/XT	30 min run	50 min	off	15 miles
Week 11						
off	40 min run	off/XT	30 min run	50 min	off	4 x 1 mile
Week 12						
off	60 min run	off/XT	30 min run	50 min	off	17 miles
Week 13						
off	40 min run	off/XT	30 min run	60 min	off	6 x 1 mile
Week 14						
off	60 min run	off/XT	30 min run	60 min	off	8 miles MM
Week 15						
off	65 min run	off/XT	30 min run	60 min	off	20 miles

Week 16

off	45 min run	off/XT	30 min run	50 min	off	10 x 1 mile

Week 17

off	65 min run	off/XT	30 min run	65 min	off	7 miles MM

Week 18

off	65 min run	off/XT	30 min run	60 min	off	23 miles

Week 19

off	45 min run	off/XT	30 min run	60 min	off	10 x 1 mile

Week 20

off	60 min run	off/XT	30 min run	65 min	off	7 miles MM

Week 21

off	60 min run	off/XT	30 min run	60 min	off	26 miles

Week 22

off	45 min run	off/XT	30 min run	65 min	off	6 miles

Week 23

off	60 min run	off/XT	30 min run	60 min	off	12 x 1 mile

Week 24

off	60 min run	off/XT	30 min run	65 min	off	7 miles MM

Week 25

off	60 min run	off/XT	30 min run	60 min	off	29 miles

Week 26

off	60 min run	off/XT	30 min run	65 min	off	6 miles

Week 27

off	60 min run	off/XT	30 min run	60 min	off	14 x 1 mile

Week 28

off	45 min run	off/XT	30 min run	60 min	off	7 miles

Week 29

off	40 min run	off/XT	30 min run	30 min	off	Goal Race/Boston

Week 30 (Recovery week)

off/XT	30 min run	off/XT	30 min run	off	5 miles	off

Time goal 5:10

Note: This is the minimum that I've found necessary to prepare for the goal. If you are already running more than this amount, and are able to recover between workouts, you may continue to do what you are doing—but be careful.

1. To begin this program, you should have run a long run within the past 2 weeks of at least 6 miles. If your long run is not this long, then gradually increase the weekend run to this distance before starting the program.

2. If your current long run is longer than 7 miles, it is possible to start on the week with a long run that is at or slightly longer than the distance of the longest run you have run in the past 2 weeks. For example, if you ran 13 miles two weeks ago, you could start with week # 8, # 9 or # 10. In this case, you will lose the benefits from the hill workouts on the short mileage weekends.

3. What is your current level of performance? The "magic mile" time trials, noted by MM on the schedule, will tell you. Read the chapter in this book on "Choosing the Right Goal..." Take your current MM and multiply by 1.3. This predicts your best possible per mile performance in the marathon under ideal conditions when you've done all of the training. Follow the instructions in that chapter to set a realistic goal and to monitor your progress. The MM is run once on each weekend noted in the schedule. You can run any pace you wish for the remaining miles assigned on these workouts. To predict a 5:10 marathon performance, your MM should be 9:05 or faster by the end of the program.

4. What pace should I run on the long runs? Take your current performance level (MM x 1.3) and add 2 minutes. The result is your suggested long run pace per mile on long runs at 60F or cooler. For those who are currently predicting a 5:10 in the marathon, the long run pace should be no faster than 14:00/mile at 60F and 15:00/mi at 70F. It is always better to run slower to ensure faster recovery.

5. On long runs, and in the marathon itself, slow down even more when the temperature rises: by 30 seconds a mile for every 5 degrees above 60F.

6. Run-Walk-Run ratio should correspond to the pace used (See the Run-Walk-Run chapter in this book).

7. Most runners don't improve more than 30 seconds per mile during a 30-week marathon training program. If your goal is more aggressive, you may increase injury stress during the training or may be frustrated with your final time. Use the MMs as reality checks on your current performance level, and remember that they are based upon "ideal projections."

8. Speed repetitions of 1 mile each are listed on the schedule for this goal. During each mile repeat, take a 30 second walk break after 2 minutes of running. Run the first and the last mile repeat in 11:45, and the others in 11:25. Stay smooth. If you are struggling to maintain pace, slow down to run efficiently. If you are slowing down significantly during the second half, shift to running twice as many 800 meter repeats. Be sure to read the section in this book on speed training.

9. Warm up for each mile repeat workout by walking for 2-5 minutes, then jog very slowly for 5-10 minutes. Next, do 4-8 acceleration-gliders (see the segment about this in this book). Reverse this process as you warm down, leaving out the acceleration gliders.

10. Recover between each mile repeat by walking and jogging for 5 minutes between each. You may choose the amount of walking vs. jogging. If you are using a heart monitor, your heart rate should drop below 65 % of max heart rate before starting another mile repeat.

11. If you have recovered from the weekend run, during your Tuesday workout run 2-4 miles at race pace (noted as "p" on the Tue line). After an easy warm-up, run 4 of the acceleration-gliders (Acg). (These are described in the drill section of this book). Then run a mile segment at 12:00, and run a second mile with a total time of 24:00, and continue at the same pace per mile for 1-2 more miles. From the beginning of these segments, take a 1 minute walk break after running for 2 minutes (2-1). This means that you will have to pick up the pace by a few seconds per minute to maintain your 12:00 pace by the watch. Stay smooth and try to maintain the same pace. This trains you to run at race pace, taking walk breaks.

12. It is fine to do cross training on Monday and Friday, if you wish. Except for running in the water, cross training doesn't tend to improve performance. Avoid exercises like stair machines (during rest days from running) that use the calf muscles.

13. Be sure to take a vacation from strenuous exercise the day before your long runs and mile repetitions.

14. On Friday, run a few hill repeats (h), as described in the hill section in this book. The Acg's will get the legs warmed up for the hill accelerations. The length of the hills should be 150 meters to 200 meters. Walk down most of each hill for almost complete recovery.

15. Hills (h) are suggested on short mileage weekends, during the early weeks of the program. Start with 2 hill repeats and increase by one hill on each successive workout until you reach 5 hills, as noted on the schedule. Because Boston has some significant hills in strategic locations, these workouts are crucial. The hills are embedded into the total mileage for the day.

16. Double workouts can be run on Tuesday and Friday. See the chapter in this book called "For Extra Credit."

17. During the last two weeks of the program, you cannot improve performance so avoid running too fast. On some of the short mile days, however, it is OK to run a 2 mile segment running 12:00 pace, while taking a 1 minute walk break after running for 2 minutes. This fine-tunes your pace judgment and your mental focus.

18. Never run through pain—read the chapter on injuries if you sense that you have the beginning of an injury.

Mon	Tue (CDAcg/p)	Wed	Thurs (CD)	Fri (Acg/h)	Sat	Sun
Week 1						
off	40 min run	off or XT	30 min run	40 min	off	7 miles
Week 2						
off	40 min run	off/XT	30 min run	40 min	off	8 miles
Week 3						
off	40 min run	off/XT	30 min run	40 min	off	5 mi with 2 hills
Week 4						
off	40 min run	off/XT	30 min run	40 min	off	9.5 miles
Week 5						
off	40 min run	off/XT	30 min run	45 min	off	5 mi with 3 hills
Week 6						
off	45 min run	off/XT	30 min run	45 min	off	11 miles
Week 7						
off	45 min run	off/XT	30 min run	45 min	off	6 mi with 4 hills
Week 8						
off	45 min run	off/XT	30 min run	45 min	off	13 miles
Week 9						
off	45 min run	off/XT	30 min run	50 min	off	6 mi with 5 hills
Week 10						
off	45 min run	off/XT	30 min run	50 min	off	15 miles
Week 11						
off	50 min run	off/XT	30 min run	50 min	off	4 x 1 mile
Week 12						
off	50 min run	off/XT	30 min run	50 min	off	17 miles
Week 13						
off	40 min run	off/XT	30 min run	60 min	off	6 x 1 mile
Week 14						
off	50 min run	off/XT	30 min run	60 min	off	8 miles MM
Week 15						
off	50 min run	off/XT	30 min run	60 min	off	20 miles

Week 16						
off	45 min run	off/XT	30 min run	50 min	off	10 x 1 mile
Week 17						
off	50 min run	off/XT	30 min run	60 min	off	7 miles MM
Week 18						
off	60 min run	off/XT	30 min run	60 min	off	23 miles
Week 19						
off	45 min run	off/XT	30 min run	60 min	off	10 x 1 mile
Week 20						
off	45 min run	off/XT	30 min run	65 min	off	7 miles MM
Week 21						
off	60 min run	off/XT	30 min run	60 min	off	26 miles
Week 22						
off	40 min run	off/XT	30 min run	60 min	off	6 miles
Week 23						
off	60 min run	off/XT	30 min run	50 min	off	12 x 1 mile
Week 24						
off	40 min run	off/XT	30 min run	60 min	off	7 miles MM
Week 25						
off	60 min run	off/XT	30 min run	50 min	off	29 miles
Week 26						
off	40 min run	off/XT	30 min run	65 min	off	6 miles
Week 27						
off	40 min run	off/XT	30 min run	50 min	off	14 x 1 mile
Week 28						
off	40 min run	off/XT	30 min run	60 min	off	7 miles
Week 29						
off	40 min run	off/XT	30 min run	30 min	off	Goal Race/Boston
Week 30 (Recovery week)						
off/XT	30 min run	off/XT	30 min run	off	5 miles	off

Time goal 5:25

Note: This is the minimum that I've found necessary to prepare for the goal. If you are already running more than this amount, and are able to recover between workouts, you may continue to do what you are doing—but be careful.

1. To begin this program, you should have run a long run within the past 2 weeks of at least 6 miles. If your long run is not this long, then gradually increase the weekend run to this distance before starting the program.

2. If your current long run is longer than 7 miles, it is possible to start on the week with a long run that is at or slightly longer than the distance of the longest run you have run in the past 2 weeks. For example, if you ran 13 miles two weeks ago, you could start with week # 8, # 9 or # 10. In this case, you will lose the benefits from the hill workouts on the short mileage weekends.

3. What is your current level of performance? The "magic mile" time trials, noted by MM on the schedule, will tell you. Read the chapter in this book on "Choosing the Right Goal..." Take your current MM and multiply by 1.3. This predicts your best possible per mile performance in the marathon under ideal conditions when you've done all of the training. Follow the instructions in that chapter to set a realistic goal and to monitor your progress. The MM is run once on each weekend noted in the schedule. You can run any pace you wish for the remaining miles assigned on these workouts. To predict a 5:25 marathon performance, your MM should be 9:25 or faster by the end of the program.

4. What pace should I run on the long runs? Take your current performance level (MM x 1.3) and add 2 minutes. The result is your suggested long run pace per mile on long runs at 60F or cooler. For those who are currently predicting a 5:25 in the marathon, the long run pace should be no faster than 14:40/mile at 60F and 15:40/mi at 70F. It is always better to run slower to ensure faster recovery.

5. On long runs, and in the marathon itself, slow down even more when the temperature rises: by 30 seconds a mile for every 5 degrees above 60F.

6. Run-Walk-Run ratio should correspond to the pace used (See the Run-Walk-Run chapter in this book).

7. Most runners don't improve more than 30 seconds per mile during a 30-week marathon training program. If your goal is more aggressive, you may increase injury stress during the training or may be frustrated with your final time. Use the MMs as reality checks on your current performance level, and remember that they are based upon "ideal projections."

8. Speed repetitions of 1 mile each are listed on the schedule for this goal. During each mile repeat, take a 30 second walk break after 2 minutes of running. Run the first and the last mile repeat in 12:15, and the others in 11:55. Stay smooth. If you are struggling to maintain pace, slow down to run efficiently. If you are slowing down significantly during the second half, shift to running twice as many 800 meter repeats. Be sure to read the section in this book on speed training.

9. Warm up for each mile repeat workout by walking for 2-5 minutes, then jog very slowly for 5-10 minutes. Next, do 4-8 acceleration-gliders (see the segment about this in this book). Reverse this process as you warm down, leaving out the acceleration gliders.

10. Recover between each mile repeat by walking and jogging for 5 minutes between each. You may choose the amount of walking vs. jogging. If you are using a heart monitor, your heart rate should drop below 65 % of max heart rate before starting another mile repeat.

11. If you have recovered from the weekend run, during your Tuesday workout run 2-4 miles at race pace (noted as "p" on the Tue line). After an easy warm-up, run 4 of the acceleration-gliders (Acg). (These are described in the drill section of this book). Then run a mile segment at 12:30, and run a second mile with a total time of 25:00, and continue at the same pace per mile for 1-2 more miles. From the beginning of these segments, take a 1 minute walk break after running for 2 minutes (or run for a minute and walk for 30 seconds). This means that you will have to pick up the pace by a few seconds per minute to maintain your 12:30 pace by the watch. Stay smooth and try to maintain the same pace. This trains you to run at race pace, taking walk breaks.

12. It is fine to do cross training on Monday and Friday, if you wish. Except for running in the water, cross training doesn't tend to improve performance. Avoid exercises like stair machines (during rest days from running) that use the calf muscles.

13. Be sure to take a vacation from strenuous exercise the day before your long runs and mile repetitions.

14. On Friday, run a few hill repeats (h), as described in the hill section in this book. The Acg's will get the legs warmed up for the hill accelerations. The length of the hills should be 150 meters to 200 meters. Walk down most of each hill for almost complete recovery.

15. Hills (h) are suggested on short mileage weekends, during the early weeks of the program. Start with 2 hill repeats and increase by one hill on each successive workout until you reach 5 hills, as noted on the schedule. Because Boston has some significant hills in strategic locations, these workouts are crucial. The hills are embedded into the total mileage for the day.

16. Double workouts can be run on Tuesday and Friday. See the chapter in this book called "For Extra Credit."

17. During the last two weeks of the program, you cannot improve performance so avoid running too fast. On some of the short mile days, however, it is OK to run a 2 mile segment running 12:30 pace, while taking a 1 minute walk break after running for 2 minutes. This fine-tunes your pace judgment and your mental focus.

18. Never run through pain—read the chapter on injuries if you sense that you have the beginning of an injury.

Mon	Tue (CDAcg/p)	Wed	Thurs (CD)	Fri (Acg/h)	Sat	Sun
Week 1						
off	40 min run	off or XT	30 min run	40 min	off	7 miles
Week 2						
off	40 min run	off/XT	30 min run	40 min	off	8 miles
Week 3						
off	40 min run	off/XT	30 min run	40 min	off	5 mi with 2 hills
Week 4						
off	40 min run	off/XT 3	0 min run	40 min	off	9.5 miles
Week 5						
off	40 min run	off/XT	30 min run	45 min	off	5 mi with 3 hills
Week 6						
off	45 min run	off/XT	30 min run	45 min	off	11 miles
Week 7						
off	45 min run	off/XT	30 min run	45 min	off	6 mi with 4 hills
Week 8						
off	45 min run	off/XT	30 min run	45 min	off	13 miles
Week 9						
off	45 min run	off/XT	30 min run	50 min	off	6 mi with 5 hills
Week 10						
off	45 min run	off/XT	30 min run	50 min	off	15 miles
Week 11						
off	50 min run	off/XT	30 min run	50 min	off	4 x 1 mile
Week 12						
off	50 min run	off/XT	30 min run	50 min	off	17 miles
Week 13						
off	40 min run	off/XT	30 min run	60 min	off	6 x 1 mile
Week 14						
off	50 min run	off/XT	30 min run	60 min	off	8 miles MM
Week 15						
off	50 min run	off/XT	30 min run	60 min	off	20 miles

Week 16

off	45 min run	off/XT	30 min run	50 min	off	10 x 1 mile

Week 17

off	50 min run	off/XT	30 min run	60 min	off	7 miles MM

Week 18

off	60 min run	off/XT	30 min run	60 min	off	23 miles

Week 19

off	45 min run	off/XT	30 min run	60 min	off	10 x 1 mile

Week 20

off	45 min run	off/XT	30 min run	65 min	off	7 miles MM

Week 21

off	60 min run	off/XT	30 min run	60 min	off	26 miles

Week 22

off	40 min run	off/XT	30 min run	60 min	off	6 miles

Week 23

off 6	0 min run	off/XT	30 min run	50 min	off	12 x 1 mile

Week 24

off	40 min run	off/XT	30 min run	60 min	off	7 miles MM

Week 25

off	60 min run	off/XT	30 min run	50 min	off	29 miles

Week 26

off	40 min run	off/XT	30 min run	65 min	off	6 miles

Week 27

off	40 min run	off/XT	30 min run	50 min	off	14 x 1 mile

Week 28

off	40 min run	off/XT	30 min run	60 min	off	7 miles

Week 29

off	40 min run	off/XT	30 min run	30 min	off	Goal Race/Boston

Week 30 (Recovery week)

off/XT	30 min run	off/XT	30 min run	off	5 miles	off

10 What If?

Making Adjustments Due to Non-perfect Conditions

Almost everyone has interruptions and scheduling problems. By using your journal to plan workouts, you can make the changes needed, gaining a great deal of control over your training. Even more important, when experiencing injury or disappointment, you can analyze data in the journal, discover problems and make changes. Here are some common problems, with solutions:

Race weekend doesn't match up with the training plan

Count back from your goal race. Try to leave 3 or 4 weeks between the race and the last long run, and 3-4 weeks between the 26 mile run and the 29 mile run.

If race day conditions are not right ...

Because of factors beyond your control, such as temperatures above 60F (14C), infection, etc., the original race day may not be the venue for your best effort. The best option, if you are not sick or injured, is to run that marathon as a training run—at least 2 min/mi slower than the "magic mile" times are predicting in an all out marathon. Add 3 more miles as a warm down and you will be ready to race again in 3 or 4 weeks. Repeat the last 3 or 4 weeks of the schedule, in this case.

Injury interruption

Top priority is to let the injury heal to the point that you can continue with training. Most injuries allow for easy running before total healing has occurred. When you have questions about this, talk to your doctor.

Speedwork puts a much greater stress on a weak link. Before restarting your speed training, you need the best advice possible from your medical team. Even then, you will need to start back conservatively:

1. When given clearance to start back, run a very easy running week or two to get your legs, tendons, etc. working together again.

2. When given clearance, and the injured area seems ready, do a "test speed workout." Warm up thoroughly and then run only 2-3 repetitions, running each slower than you were running before the injury, with more rest than you would usually take.

3. If there are no problems from this test, then ease back into the training on the schedule.

4. Most injury interruptions will take 2-3 weeks of transition to get you back on the plan. If you had a week or more off from running, it may take more time to get back on plan.

5. Use your journal to add weeks to the plan, and schedule another marathon. You may be able to run the original marathon as a training run—if you can slow down by at least 2 min/mi slower than the pace you could run all-out.

6. Be sensitive to your "weak link" that was injured.

Sickness interruption

Top priority is to ensure that you are not going to pull your resistance further down by returning to running. If there is a lung infection, don't run, and get clearance from your doctor before starting back. Lung infections will also have a longer term effect on your strength, requiring more time to transition back to running. When you and the doctor feel that you can resume training, ease back as follows:

1. Run a very easy running week or two, with liberal walk breaks, to get legs, tendons, etc. working together again.

2. When given medical clearance for speedwork, and you feel up to it, do a "test speed workout." Warm up thoroughly and then run only 2-3 repetitions, running each slower than you were running before the sickness, with more rest than you would usually take between each.

3. If there are no problems from this test, then ease back into the training on the schedule.

4. Most sickness interruptions will take only 1-2 weeks of transition to get back to the plan. If there is significant fatigue or lingering infection issues, talk to the doctor and take more time to come back.

5. Use your journal to add weeks to your plan. Choose another marathon, if needed.

6. Be sensitive to any signs that you may be lowering your resistance or getting another infection.

Career, vacation, family interruptions

Life will intervene several times during a year. When you did not have a sickness or injury, you need little transition time to resume the plan. It will help greatly on these "vacation from your plan" weeks to do at least 15 minutes of running, every other day. This will maintain most of your running adaptations. If you miss a speed workout, it's best to do a "make up" workout within 4 days of the date on the schedule.

Cross training can keep you fit, if you must stop running

I know of many runners who have had to take 2 weeks off from running or more, and have not lost noticeable fitness. How? They cross trained. As noted above, the most effective cross training mode is water running.

The key is to do an activity (like water running) that uses the same range of motion used in running. This keeps the neuromuscular system working to capacity.

To maintain conditioning, you must simulate the time and the effort level you would have spent when running. For example, if you were scheduled for a long run that would have taken you 60 minutes, get in the pool and run for 60 minutes. You can take segments of 30-40 seconds in which you reduce your effort (like a walk break), every few minutes, to keep the muscles resilient.

On a speed day, run water segments of about the same time you would have run for those segments on the track. Whether going long or fast, try to get up to the same approximate respiration rate that you would have felt when running.

11 The Galloway Run-Walk-Run Method

"Walk breaks give you control over your training and your fatigue."

I doubt that you will find any training component that will help you in more ways than my run-walk-run method. I continue to be amazed, every week, at the reports of how these strategic walks help runners enjoy the running experience as they improve the finish time. When placed appropriately for the individual, fatigue is erased, motivation improves, running enjoyment is enhanced, and the runner feels confident of finishing with strength. Here's how it works.

Walk before you get tired

Most of us, even when untrained, can walk for several miles before fatigue sets in, because walking is an activity that we are bio-engineered to do for hours. Running is more work, because you have to lift your body off the ground and then absorb the shock of the landing, over and over. This is why the continuous use of the running muscles will produce fatigue, aches and pains much more quickly. If you walk before your running muscles start to get tired, you allow the muscle to recover instantly—increasing your capacity for exercise while reducing the chance of next-day soreness.

The "method" concept means having a strategy. By inserting walk breaks according to your formula, you can manage fatigue, and be strong to the finish. The resurgence of the running muscles, with each walk break, bestows confidence to take on the challenges—even unknown ones. The right ratio of running and walking allows one to feel better during and after the run, with the confidence to keep pushing further.

"The run-walk-run method is very simple: you run for a short segment, take a walk break, and keep repeating this pattern."

Walk breaks allow you to take control over fatigue, in advance, so that you can enjoy every run. By walking early and often you can feel strong, even after running farther than you've ever run before. Even elite runners find that walk breaks on long runs allow them to recover faster. There is no need to be exhausted at the end of a run—even a 30 miler.

Walk Breaks...

- Give you control over the way you feel at the end.
- Erase fatigue.
- Push back your fatigue wall.
- Allow for endorphins to collect during each walk break—you feel good!
- Break up the distance into manageable units. ("I only have to run three more minutes.")
- Allow for speed recovery.
- Reduce the chance of aches, pains and injury.
- Allow you to feel good afterward—carrying on the rest of your day without debilitating fatigue.
- Give you all of the endurance of the distance of each session—without the pain.
- Allow older runners or heavier runners to recover fast, and feel as good or better than the younger (slimmer) days.

A short and gentle walking stride

It's better to walk slowly, with a short stride. There has been some irritation of the shins, when runners or walkers maintain a stride that is too long. Relax and enjoy the walk.

No need to ever eliminate the walk breaks

Some beginners assume that they must work toward the day when they don't have to take any walk breaks at all. This is up to the individual, but is not recommended. Remember that you decide what ratio of run-walk-run to use. There is no rule that requires you to hold to any ratio on a given day. As you adjust the run-walk to how you feel, you gain control over the whole experience, including the motivation to increase distance.

I've run for over 50 years, and I enjoy running more than ever because of walk breaks. Each run I take energizes my day. I would not be able to run almost every day if I didn't insert the walk breaks early and often. I start most runs taking a short walk break every minute. By 2 miles I am usually walking every 3-4 minutes. By 5 miles the ratio often goes to every 7-10 minutes. But there are days every year when I stay at 3 minutes and even a few days at 1 min.

How to keep track of the walk breaks

The best device we have found is on our website. This is a run-walk-run timer that vibrates when it's time to walk, and then vibrates when it's time to run again. Check our website (www.jeffgalloway.com) or a good running store for advice in this area.

Strategies by pace

Whether running fast or slow, for each pace, here are the ratios.

Pace/Mile	Run segment	Walk segment
5:00	10 minutes	15 seconds
5:30	5 minute	15 seconds
6:00	6 minute	20 seconds
7:00	7 minute	30 seconds
7:30	5 minutes	30 seconds
8:00	4 minutes	30 seconds
8:30	4 minutes	45 seconds
9:00	4 minutes	1 minute
9:30	3 minutes	1 minute
10:00	3 minutes	1 minute
10:30	2:30	45 seconds
11:00	2:30	1 minute
11:30	2 minutes	1 minute
12:00	2 minutes	1 minute
12:30	1:30	1 minute
13:00	1 minute	1 minute
13:30	30 seconds	30 seconds
14:00	30 seconds	30 seconds

12 The "Magic Mile" is Your Reality Check

In the early 1990s, I started using a one-mile time trial (called a "magic mile" or MM) as a reality check on current time goals. After looking at the data from thousands of runners, I've found this to be the best way to predict the best performance possible during a training program. By adding 2 min/mi to the predicted marathon pace, one can set a conservative pace on long runs that will reduce injury risk. By the end of the training program, I've found the MM to be the best predictor of an ideal, all-out pace in an upcoming race.

In order to run the time in the race indicated by the MM:
- You have done the training necessary for the goal—according to the training programs in this book.
- You are not injured.
- You run with an even-paced effort.
- The weather on goal race day is not adverse (below 60F or 14C, no strong headwinds, no heavy rain or snow, etc.).
- There are no crowds to run through, or significant hills.

The "Magic Mile" time trials (MM) are reality checks on your goal. These should be done on the weeks noted on the schedule. The MM has been the best predictor of current potential and helps to set a realistic training pace. With this information, you can decide how hard to run during various situations. (If you have any injuries you should not do the MM.)

- Warm up for these with about 10 minutes of very easy running with liberal walk breaks.
- Do 4-6 acceleration-gliders as in the book—no sprinting .
- Run around a track if at all possible (or a very accurately measured segment).
- Time yourself for 4 laps (or an accurately measured mile). Start the watch at the beginning, and keep it running until you cross the finish of the 4th lap.
- **On the first MM, don't run all-out: run at a pace that is only slightly faster than your current pace.**
- Only one MM is done on each day it is assigned.
- On each successive MM (usually 3 weeks later), your mission is to beat the previous best time.
- Don't ever push so hard that you hurt your feet, knees, etc.
- Jog slowly for the rest of the distance assigned on that day taking as many walk breaks as you wish.

- At the end of the program take your fastest MM and multiply by 1.3 to see what pace might be possible on an ideal day (without crowds).
- Long run training pace is at least two minutes per mile slower than this (MM x 1.3) pace.

After you have run 3 of these MMs (not at one time—on different weekends) you'll see progress and will run them hard enough so that you are huffing and puffing during the second half. For prediction purposes, you want to finish feeling like you couldn't go much further at that pace. Try walking for about 10-15 seconds at the half, during the MM. Some runners record a faster time when taking short breaks, and some go faster when running continuously. Do what works for you on the MM.

Galloway's Performance Predictor

Step 1: Run your "magic mile" time trial (MM) (4 laps around the track)
Step 2: Compute your mile pace for the marathon by multiplying by 1.3

Example:
Mile time: 6:00

For the best possible marathon pace, currently, multiply 6 x 1.3 = 7.8 min/mi or 7:48
For the fastest long run training pace, add 2 minutes per mile = 9:48 minutes per mile (Remember to slow down 30 sec/mile for every 5 degrees above 60F.) It's always better to go slower on the long runs.

(x 1.3) (add 2 min/mi)

One Mile Time	FAST Marathon Pace	Long Run Training Pace
5:00	6:30	8:30
5:30	7:09	9:10
6:00	7:48	9:50
6:30	8:27	10:30
7:00	9:06	11:10
7:30	9:45	11:45
8:00	10:24	12:30
8:30	11:03	13:10
9:00	11:42	13:50
9:30	12:21	14:30
10:00	13:00	15:00

Note: The "FAST Marathon Prediction" multiplier assumes that you will be running about all-out effort by the end of the marathon—under perfect conditions.

The "leap of faith" goal prediction

I have no problem allowing my e-coach athletes, who've run one or more marathons, to choose a goal time that is faster than that predicted by the MM at the beginning of a 6 month program. As you do the speed training, the long runs and your MMs, you should improve...but how much? In my experience this "leap of faith" should not exceed 5 %.

1. Run the MM time trial.
2. Use the formula above to predict the pace you could run now, if you were trained for the marathon.
3. Choose the amount of improvement during the training program (3-5 %).
4. Subtract this improvement amount from # 2—this is your goal time.

How much of a "leap of faith"?

Marathon Pre-test prediction (Over a 5-6 month training program)	* 3 % Improvement *	5 % Improvement
7:00 per mile marathon pace	6:47	6:39
8:00 per mile marathon pace	7:45	7:36
9:00 per mile marathon pace	8:43	8:33
10:00 per mile marathon pace	9:42	9:30
11:00 per mile marathon pace	10:40	10.27

Finish Time Improvement Marathon Pre-test prediction	3 %	5 %
3:00	2:54:36	2:51:00
3:30	2:23:42	3:20:00
4:00	3:52:48	3:48:00

The key to goal setting is keeping your ego in check. From my experience, I have found that a 3 % improvement is realistic. This means that if your marathon time is predicted to be 3:00, then it is realistic to assume you could lower it by five and a half minutes if you do the speed training and the long runs as noted on my training schedules in this book. The maximum improvement, which is less likely, is a more aggressive 5 % or 9 minutes off a three-hour marathon.

In both of these situations, however, everything must come together to produce the predicted result. Even runners who shoot for a 3 % improvement and do all the training as described achieve their goal slightly more than 50 % of the time during a racing season. The more aggressive performances usually result in success about 20 % of the time. There are many factors that determine a time goal in a marathon that are outside of your control: weather, terrain, infection, etc.

"Magic Mile" Time Trials (MMs) give you a reality check

1. Follow the same format as listed in the pre-test, above.
2. By doing this as noted, you will learn how to pace yourself.
3. Hint: it's better to start a bit more slowly than you think you can run.
4. Walk breaks will be helpful for most runners. Read the section in this book for suggested ratios.
5. Note whether you are speeding up or slowing down at the end, and adjust in the next MM.
6. If you are not making progress, then look for reasons and take action.

Reasons why you may not be improving:
- You're over-trained, and tired—if so, reduce your training, and/or take an extra rest day.
- You may have chosen a goal that is too ambitious for your current ability
- You may have missed some of your workouts, or not been as regular with your training as needed.
- The temperature may have been above 60F (14C). Above this, you will slow down (the longer the race, the more affect heat will make on the result).
- You ran the first lap or two too fast.

Final reality check

Take your fastest 3 MMs and average them to get a good prediction in your goal race. If the tests are predicting a time that is slower than the goal you've been training for, go with the time predicted by the "magic mile." It is strongly recommended that you run the first one-third of your goal race a few seconds per mile slower than the pace predicted by the MM average.

Use a journal!

Read the next chapter—on using a journal. Your odds of reaching your goal increase greatly with this very important instrument. Psychologically, a journal empowers you to take responsibility for the fulfillment of your mission.

13 Your Journal—The Best Planning and Evaluation Tool

This is your book

Yes, you are writing a book. You already have the outline: your weekly schedule. As you follow it, your journal will document the good times, and the slow ones. It will allow you to modify your plan and track the changes. Later, you can look back after success or disappointment and often find reasons for either. If we don't look back at the history of our setbacks, we will have a tendency to repeat them.

The various types of journals

Calendar—facing you on the wall

Many runners start recording their runs on a wall calendar—or one that is posted on the refrigerator. Looking at the miles recorded is empowering. But equally motivating for many is seeing too many "zeros" on days that should have been running days. If you're not sure whether you will really get into this journal process, you may find it easiest to start with a calendar.

An organized running journal

When you use a product that is designed for running, you don't have to think to record the facts. The spaces on the page ask you for certain info, and you will learn to fill it very quickly. This leaves you time to use some of the open space for the creative thoughts and ideas that pop out during a run. Look at the various journals available and pick one that looks to be easier to use, and to carry with you. I've included a sample page of my Jeff Galloway Training Journal (available at **www.JeffGalloway.com**).

Week of | Jan 1

Thursday

GOAL	35 min easy (SC)	
TIME	45 min	
DISTANCE	@ 6.5	
AM PULSE	49	
WEATHER	Cloudy	
TEMP	40°	
TIME	6	AM PM
TERRAIN	rolling	
DATE	WALK BREAK —	

Jan 4

COMMENTS

Great run with Barb, Wes + Sambo — who took out the pace too fast + died at the end. The rest of us caught up on the gossip. Achilles ached so I iced it for 15 minutes.

1 2 3 4 5 6 7 ⑧ 9 10

Friday

GOAL	45 min (SP) 5 x 800 meter	
TIME	1:15	
DISTANCE	7.5 mi	
AM PULSE	53	
WEATHER	45°	
TEMP	Sunny	
TIME	5	AM PM
TERRAIN	track	
DATE	WALK BREAK 400 m	

Jan 5

COMMENTS

2:30   My best workout in years!
2:36   - walked 400m between each
2:33   - struggled on last one
2:37
2:32
2:36   Achilles ached - iced 15 min
12 min warm up and warm down

1 2 3 4 ⑤ felt 6 7 Perform ⑧ 9 10

Saturday

GOAL	Off	
TIME		
DISTANCE		
AM PULSE	55	
WEATHER		
TEMP		
TIME		AM PM
TERRAIN		
DATE	WALK BREAK	

Jan 6

COMMENTS

Kids soccer (Morn)
* Westin scores goal bouncing off his back
   1st goal of season!
   Brennan's cross country (aft)
      Invitational
* Brennan comes from 8th to 3rd in
   the last half mile. I'm so proud!

1 2 3 4 5 6 7 8 9 10

Sunday

GOAL	18 mi (1) easy!	
TIME	2:53	
DISTANCE	18 mi	
AM PULSE	52	
WEATHER	50°	
TEMP	dry no wind	
TIME		AM PM
TERRAIN	flat	
DATE	WALK BREAK 1 min / mi	

Jan 7

COMMENTS

It was great to cover 18 miles —
wish I had a group
longest run in 18 months!
      but...
* went too fast in the first 5 miles
* Achilles hurt afterward - take 3 days
* Power Bar + water from 10 mi kept spirits up

1 2 3 4 5 ⑥ 7 8 9 10

* Pulse is up — I'm not recovering - need more days off/week

Notebook

You don't need to have a commercial product. You can create your own journal by using a basic school notebook, of your choice. Find one of the sizes that works best with your lifestyle (briefcase, purse, etc.) Below you will find the items that I've found helpful for most runners to record. But the best journals are those that make it easier for you to collect the data you find interesting, while allowing for creativity. The non-limiting nature of a notebook is a more comfortable format for runners that like to write a lot one day, and not so much another day.

Computer Logs

There are a growing number of electronic devices (mostly GPS) that allow you to sort through information more quickly. As you set up your own codes and sections you can pick data that is important to you, sort it to see trends and plan ahead.

The planning process

1. Look over the full training schedule and make any changes needed to customize it for your use.

2. Write down the goal races on the appropriate weeks in your journal. Take a highlighter or other method to make these weeks stand out.

3. Write down the assigned workouts for each day of each week for the next 8 weeks in pencil.

4. Look at each of the next 8 weeks quickly to make sure you don't have any trips, meetings or family responsibilities that require adjusting the workouts.

5. Each week, add another week's workouts in pencil, and note any changes in your travel, etc. schedule.

6. Each week, look ahead carefully at the next two weeks to ensure that the workouts are adjusted to your real life schedule.

The Data Recording

1. As soon as you can, after a run, write the facts in your journal:

- mileage
- pace
- repetitions—times
- rest interval
- aches or pains—specifically where and how they hurt
- problems

In addition, you may also record:

Time of run:

Total time running:

Weather:

Temp_____

Precipitation_____

Humidity_____

Walk-Run frequency

Any special segments of the run (speed, hills, race, etc.)

Running companion

Terrain

How did you feel (1-10)

Comments:

2. Go back over the list again and fill in more details—emotional responses, changes in energy or blood sugar level and location of places where you had aches and pains—even if they went away during the run. You are looking for patterns of items that could indicate injury, blood sugar problems, lingering fatigue, etc.

3. Helpful additions (usually in a blank section at the bottom of the page)
- Improvement thoughts
- Things I should have done differently

- Interesting happenings
- Funny things
- Strange things
- Stories, right brain crazy thoughts

Your morning pulse is a great guide of overstress

Recording morning pulse—immediately upon waking

1. As soon as you are conscious—but before you have thought much about anything—count your pulse rate for a minute. Record it before you forget it. If you don't have your journal by your bed, then keep a piece of paper and a pen handy.

2. It is natural for there to be some fluctuations, based upon the time you wake up, how long you have been awake, etc. But after several weeks and months, these will balance themselves out. The ideal would be to catch the pulse at the instant that you are awake, before the shock of an alarm clock, thoughts of work stress, etc.

3. After 2 weeks or so of readings, you can establish a baseline morning pulse. Take out the top 2 high readings and then average the readings.

4. The average is your guide. If the rate is 5 % higher than your average, take an easy day. When the rate is 10 % higher, and there is no reason for this (you woke up from an exciting dream, medication, infection, etc.), then your muscles may be tired indeed. Take the day off if you have a walk-run scheduled for that day.

5. If your pulse stays high for more than a week, call your doctor to see if there is a reason for this (medication, hormones, metabolic changes, infection, etc.). This could be due to overtraining.

14 Form Improvement Drills—To Make Running Faster and Easier

The following drills have helped thousands of runners run more efficiently and faster. Each develops different capabilities, and each rewards the individual for running smoother, reducing impact, using momentum, and increasing the cadence or turnover of feet and legs. With each drill, you'll be teaching yourself to move more directly and easily down the road.

When?

These should be done on a non-long run day. It is fine, however, to insert them into your warm-up, before a race or a speed workout. Many runners have also told me that the drills are a nice way to break up an average run that otherwise might be called "boring."

CD—The Cadence Drill for faster turnover

This is an easy drill that helps you to become a smoother runner, using less effort. By doing it regularly, you pull all the elements of good running form together at the same time. One drill a week will help you step lightly, as you increase the number of steps you take per minute. This will help you run faster, with less effort.

1. Warm up by walking for 5 minutes, and running and walking very gently for 10 minutes.

2. Start jogging slowly for 1-2 minutes, and then time yourself for 30 seconds. During this half minute, count the number of times your left foot touches.

3. Walk around for a minute or so.

4. On the 2nd 30 second drill, increase the count by 1 or 2.

5. Repeat this 3-7 more times, each time trying to increase by 1-2 additional counts.

In the process of improving turnover, the body's internal monitoring system coordinates a series of adaptations which make the feet, legs, nervous system and timing mechanism work together as an efficient team:

- Your foot touches more gently.
- Extra, inefficient motions of the foot and leg are reduced or eliminated.
- Less effort is spent on pushing up or moving forward.
- You stay lower to the ground.
- The ankle becomes more efficient.
- Ache and pain areas are not overused.

Acceleration-Glider Drills

This drill is a very easy and gentle form of speed play, or fartlek. By doing it regularly, you develop a range of speeds, with the muscle conditioning to move smoothly from one to the next. The greatest benefit comes as you learn how to "glide," or coast off your momentum.

1. Done on a non-long-run day, in the middle of a shorter run, or as a warm-up for a speed session or a race—or MM day.

2. Warm up with at least half a mile of easy running.

3. Many runners do the cadence drill just after the easy warm-up, followed by the acceleration-gliders. But each can be done separately, if desired.

4. Run 4-8 of them.

5. Do this at least once a week.

6. No sprinting—never run all-out.

After teaching this drill at my one-day running schools and weekend retreats for years, I can say that most people learn better through practice when they work on the concepts listed below—rather than the details—of the drill. So just get out there and try them!

Gliding—The most important concept. This is like coasting off the momentum of a downhill run. You can do some of your gliders running down a hill if you want, but it is important to do at least two of them on the flat land.

Do this every week—As in the cadence drills, regularity is very important. If you're like most runners, you won't glide very far at first. Regular practice will help you glide farther and farther.

Don't sweat the small stuff—I've included a general guideline of how many steps to do with each part of the drill, but don't worry about getting any set number of steps. It's best to get into a flow with this drill and not worry at all about how many steps you are taking.

Smooth transition—between each of the components. Each time you "shift gears" you are using the momentum of the current mode to start you into the next mode. Don't make a sudden and abrupt change, but have a smooth transition between modes.

Here's how it's done:

- Start by jogging very slowly for about 15 steps.
- Then, jog faster for about 15 steps—increasing to a regular running pace for you.
- Now, over the next fifteen steps, gradually increase the speed to your current race pace.
- OK, it's time to glide, or coast. Allow yourself to gradually slow down to a jog using momentum as long as you can. At first you may only glide for 10-20 steps. As the months go by you will get up to 30 and beyond... you're gliding!

Overall Purpose: As you do this drill, every week, your form will become smoother at each mode of running. Congratulations! You are learning how to keep moving at a fairly fast pace without using much energy. This is the main object of the drill.

There will be some weeks when you will glide longer than others—don't worry about this. By doing this drill regularly, you will find yourself coasting or gliding down the smallest of inclines, and even for 10-20 yards on the flat, on a regular basis. Gliding conserves energy—reduces soreness, fatigue, while helping you to maintain a faster race pace.

15 The Principles of Great Running Form

After having analyzed over 10 thousand runners in my running schools and weekend retreats, I've found that most runners are running very close to their ideal efficiency. The mistakes are seldom big ones. But a series of small mistakes can slow you down or create major aches, pains and sometimes injuries. By making a few minor adjustments, most runners can feel better and run faster.

Faster runners tend to make mistakes that cost them seconds and sometimes minutes in races. Before I detail these common problems, let's look at some principles of running form.

I believe that running is an inertial activity

This means that your primary missions are 1) to maintain momentum, an 2) to conserve resources. Very little strength is needed to run—even to run fast for short races like the 800 meters. During the first hundred meters you'll get your body into the motion and rhythm for your run. After that, the best strategy is to conserve energy while maintaining that forward momentum. To reduce fatigue, aches and pains, your right brain, helped by muscle memory, intuitively fine-tunes your mechanics and motion to minimize effort.

Humans have many biomechanical adaptations working for them, which have been made more efficient over more than a million years of walking and running. The anatomical running efficiency of the human body originates in the ankle and Achilles tendon—which I treat as a unit. This is no average body part, however, but an extremely sophisticated system of levers, springs, balancing devices and more. Biomechanics experts believe that this degree of development was not needed for walking. When our ancient ancestors had to run to survive, the ankle/Achilles adapted to endurance running/walking producing a masterpiece of bioengineering.

Through a series of speed sessions and drills, you can maximize use of the Achilles and ankle so that a very little amount of muscle work produces a quicker, consistent forward movement. During the first few speed sessions your legs may be a little sore. But as you get in better and better shape, with improved endurance, you'll find yourself going farther and faster with little or no increased effort. Other muscle groups offer support and help to fine-tune the process. When you feel aches and pains that might be due to the way you run, going back to the minimal use of the ankle and Achilles tendon can often leave you feeling smooth and efficient very quickly.

Three negative results of inefficient form:

1. Fatigue from extraneous motions becomes so severe that it takes much longer to recover.
2. Muscles or tendons are pushed so far beyond their limits that they break down and become injured—or just hurt.
3. The experience is so negative, that the desire to run is reduced, producing burnout.

Wobbling: It all starts with general fatigue that stresses your weak links. For example, if your calf muscles become fatigued at the end of a workout or a race, and you keep pushing to maintain pace, your body will use other muscles and tendons to keep going. You start to "wobble" as these alternatives are not designed to do the job, stressing the knees, hips, back, glutes, hamstrings, etc. The longer you "wobble," the more prone you are to injury.

Stride extension when tired: There are several instincts that can hurt us. When tired, for example, many runners try to extend stride length to maintain pace. This may work for a while—at the expense of the quads, hamstrings, and several other components that are over-stressed. It is always better, when you feel even a slight aggravation at the end of a run, to cut stride, and get back into a smooth motion. It's OK to push through tiredness when running smoothly as long as you are not feeling pain in any area. But if this means extending stride or wobbling (which aggravates your weak links) you will pay for this.

Be sensitive and avoid irritation: I don't suggest that everyone try to create perfect form. But when you become aware of your form problems, and make changes to become more efficient, you'll reduce aches and pains, run smoother, reduce fatigue, and run faster, over time.

Relaxed muscles—especially at the end of the run

Overall, the running motion should feel smooth, and there should be no tension in your neck, back, shoulders or legs. Even during the last half mile of a hard workout or race, try to maintain the three main elements of good form, and you'll stay relaxed: upright posture, feet low to the ground, and relaxed stride. You should not try to push through tightness and pain. Adjust your form to reduce aches and recovery time.

The big three: posture, stride and bounce

In thousands of individual running form consultations, I've discovered that when runners have problems, they tend to occur in these three areas. Often the problems are like a signature—tending to be very specific to the areas that you overuse, because of your unique movement patterns. By making a few small changes in your running form, you can reduce or eliminate the source of the problems—the source of the pain.

I. Posture

Good running posture is actually good body posture. The head is naturally balanced over the shoulders, which are aligned over the hips. As the foot comes underneath, all of these elements are in balance so that no energy is needed to prop up the body. You shouldn't have to work to pull a wayward body back from a wobble or an inefficient motion.

Forward lean—the most common mistake

The posture errors tend to be mostly due to a forward lean—especially when we are tired. The head wants to get to the finish as soon as possible, but the legs can't go any faster. A common tendency at the end of a speed session is to lean with the head. In races, this results in more than a few falls around the finish line. A forward lean will often concentrate fatigue, soreness and tightness in the lower back, or neck. Biomechanics experts note that a forward lean will reduce stride length, causing a slowdown and/or an increase in effort.

It all starts with the head. When the neck muscles are relaxed, the head can naturally seek an alignment that is balanced on the shoulders. If there is tension in the neck, or soreness afterward, the head is usually leaning too far forward. This triggers a more general upper body imbalance in which the head and chest are suspended slightly ahead of the hips and feet. Sometimes, headaches result from this postural problem. Ask a running companion to tell you if and when your head is too far forward, or leaning down. This usually occurs at the end of a tiring run. The ideal position of the head is mostly upright, with your eyes focused about 30-40 yards ahead of you. Imagine that you are a "puppet on a string."

Sitting back

The hips are the other major postural component that can easily get out of alignment. A runner with this problem, when observed from the side, will have the butt behind the rest of the body. When the pelvic area is shifted back, the legs are not allowed to go through their ideal range of motion, and the stride length is shortened. This produces a slower pace, even when spending significant effort. Many runners tend to hit harder on their heels when their hips are shifted back—but this is not always the case.

A backward lean is rare

It is rare for runners to lean back, but it happens. In my experience, this is usually due to a structural problem in the spine or hips. If you do this, and you're having pain in the neck, back or hips, you should see an orthopedist that specializes in the back. One symptom is excessive shoe wear on the back of the heel—but there are other reasons why you may show this kind of wear.

Correction: "Puppet on a string"

The best correction I've found to postural problems has been this mental image exercise: imagine that you are a puppet on a string. In other words, you're suspended from above like a puppet—from the head and each side of the shoulders. In this way, your head lines up above the shoulders, the hips come directly underneath, and the feet naturally touch lightly—directly underneath. It won't hurt anyone to do the "puppet" several times during a run.

It helps to combine this image with a deep breath. About every 4-5 minutes, as you start to run after a walk break, take a deep, lower lung breath, straighten up and say "I'm a puppet." Then imagine that you don't have to spend energy maintaining this upright posture, because the "strings" attached from above keep you on track. As you continue to use this visualization, you reinforce good posture, and the behavior can become a good habit.

Upright posture not only allows you to stay relaxed, you will probably improve stride length. When you lean forward, you'll be cutting your stride to stay balanced. When you straighten up, you'll receive a stride bonus of an inch or so, without any increase in energy.

Note: Don't try to increase stride length. When it happens naturally, you won't feel it—you'll just run faster.

An oxygen dividend

Breathing improves when you straighten up. A leaning body can't get ideal use out of the lower lungs. This can cause side pain. When you run upright, the lower lungs can receive adequate air, maximize oxygen absorption and reduce the chance of side pain.

Note: Over the years, I've found a handful of runners who naturally run with a forward lean. If this is the way you've run and don't have any back, neck or other problems, continue. Each person should run the way that is natural and most run upright, according to my experience.

II. Feet low to the ground

The most efficient stride is a shuffle—with feet close to the ground. As long as you pick your foot up enough to avoid stumbling over a rock or uneven pavement, stay low. Most runners don't need to get more than 1" clearance—even when running fast. As you increase speed, and ankle action, you will come off the ground a bit more than this. Again, don't try to increase stride, let this happen naturally.

Your ankle combined with your Achilles tendon will act as a spring, moving you forward with each running step. If you stay low to the ground, very little effort is required. Through this "shuffling" technique, running becomes almost automatic. When runners err on bounce, they try to push off too hard. This usually results in extra effort spent in lifting the body off the ground. You can think of this as energy wasted in the air—energy that could be used to run faster at the end, when it counts.

The other negative force that penalizes those who bounce too much is that of gravity. The higher you rise, the harder you fall. Each additional bounce off the ground delivers a lot more impact on feet and legs—which during speed sessions, races, and long runs, produces aches, pains and injuries.

The correction for too much bounce: Light Touch

The ideal foot "touch" should be so light that you don't usually feel yourself pushing off or landing. This means that your foot stays low to the ground and goes though an efficient and natural motion. Instead of trying to overcome gravity, you get in synch with it. If your foot "slaps" when you run, you will definitely improve with a lighter touch.

Here's a "light touch drill": During the middle of a run, time yourself for 20 seconds. Focus on one item: touching so softly that you don't hear your feet. Earplugs are not allowed for this drill. Imagine that you are running on thin ice or through a bed of hot coals. Do several of these 20-second touches, becoming quieter and quieter. You should feel very little impact on your feet as you do this drill.

III. Stride length

Studies have shown that as runners get faster, the stride length shortens. This clearly shows that the key to faster and more efficient running is increased cadence or quicker turnover of feet and legs. A major cause of aches, pains and injuries is a stride length that is too long. When in doubt, it is always better to err on the side of having a shorter stride.

Don't lift your knees!

Even most of the world-class distance runners don't have a high knee lift. When your knees go too high, you are over-using the quadriceps muscle (front of the thigh), resulting in a stride that is too long to be efficient. Many runners do this subconsciously at the end of long runs and races. This often produces sore quads for the next day or two.

Don't kick out too far in front of you!

If you watch the natural movement of the leg, it will kick forward slightly as the foot gently moves forward in the running motion and then comes underneath to contact the ground. Let this be a natural motion that produces no tightness in the muscles behind the lower or upper leg.

Tightness in the front of the shin, or behind the knee, or in the hamstring (back of the thigh) is a sign that you are kicking too far forward, and reaching out too far. Correct this by staying low to the ground, shortening the stride, and lightly touching the ground.

16 Hill Training Builds Strength—And More

Hill training strengthens the legs for running, better than any other activity I know. At the same time it can help you maximize an efficient stride length, increase leg speed, and improve your ability to run hills in races. The hill training period provides a gentle introduction to faster running, while improving your capacity to perform the speedwork later in the program. You'll also prepare for the hills on the Boston course.

You'll see on the training schedule that hills are gradually introduced into the program, while the long runs are increasing. Complete rest (by walking down the hill) is recommended after each hill so that injury risk is reduced to a very low level. A day off from running is also recommended after running hills.

The Hill Workout

- Walk for 5 minutes.
- Jog and walk to a hill—about 10 minutes. Jog a minute and walk a minute (a longer warm-up is fine).
- Do 4 acceleration-gliders. These are listed in the "Drills" chapter (don't sprint).
- Reverse this warm-up as your warm down.
- Choose a hill with a gentle grade—steep hills often cause problems and bestow no benefit.
- Walk to the top of the hill. Then step off the length of your hill segment by walking down from the top: noted on each time goal schedule.
- Mark the place after you step it off. This is where each hill starts. Walk to the bottom of the hill.
- Run up the hill for 5 seconds, and then down for 5 seconds. Walk for 10-15 seconds. Repeat this 5-10 times. This finalizes the warm-up.
- Walk for 3-4 minutes.
- Run the first few steps of each hill acceleration at a jog, then gradually pick up the turnover of the feet as you go up the hill.
- Get into a comfortable rhythm, so that you can gradually increase this rhythm or turnover (# of steps per minute) as you go up the hill.
- Keep stride length short—and keep shortening stride as you go up the hill.
- It's OK to huff and puff at the top of the hill (due to increased turnover and running uphill, but don't let the legs get over extended, or feel exhausted.
- Run over the top of the hill by at least 10 steps.
- Jog back to the top of the hill and walk down to recover between the hills. Walk as much as you need for complete recovery after each hill.

Hill Running Form

- Start with a comfortable stride—fairly short.
- As you go up the hill, shorten the stride.
- Touch lightly with your feet.
- Maintain a body posture that is perpendicular to the horizontal (upright, not leaning forward or back).
- Pick up the turnover of your feet as you go up and over the top.
- Keep adjusting stride so that the leg muscles don't tighten up—you want them as resilient as possible.
- Relax as you go over the top of the hill, and glide (or coast) a bit on the downside.

Hill training strengthens lower legs and improves running form

The incline of the hill forces your legs to work harder as you go up. The extra work up the incline and the faster turnover builds strength. By taking an easy walk between the hills, and an easy day afterward, the lower leg muscles become stronger. Over several months, the improved strength allows you to support your body weight farther forward on your feet. An extended range of motion of the ankle and Achilles tendon results in a "bonus" extension of the foot forward—with no increase in effort. You will run faster without working harder. What a deal!

Running faster on hills in races

Once you train yourself to run with efficient hill form, you'll run faster with increased turnover on the hill workouts. This prepares you to do the same in races. You won't run quite as fast in a race as in your workouts. But through hill training you can run faster than you used to run up the same hill on a race course.

Hill technique in a race is the same as in workouts: keep shortening stride as you move up the hill. Monitor your respiration rate: don't huff and puff more than you were doing on the flat. As runners improve their hill technique in races, they find that a shorter and quicker stride reduces effort while increasing speed—with no increase in breathing rate.

Note: On your long runs and easy running days, just jog up hills, don't run faster up the hill. If your breathing is increasing on a hill, reduce effort and stride length until your respiration is as it was on the flat ground.

Downhill form
- Maintain a light touch of the foot.
- Use an average stride—or quick shuffle.
- Keep feet low to the ground.
- Let gravity pull you down the hill.
- Turnover of the feet will pick up.
- Try to glide (or coast) quickly down the hill.

Biggest mistakes: too long a stride, bouncing too much

Even when the stride is one or two inches too long, your downhill speed can get out of control. If you are bouncing more than an inch or two off the ground, you run the risk of pounding your feet, having to use your quads to slow down (producing soreness) and creating hamstring soreness due to overstride. The best indicator of overstride is having tight hamstrings (big muscle at the back of your upper leg), and sore quads the next day.

17 Speed Training Prepares You for Top Performance

Getting faster requires extra work

To get faster, you must push beyond your current performance capacity. But you must be careful. Even a small amount over your speed limit can result in longer recovery or injury. The secret is to push only a little harder on each workout, then back off so the systems can rebound and improve. Gradual and gentle increases are always better because you are more likely to sustain a continuous and long-term improvement.

Our bodies are programmed to conserve resources by doing the smallest amount of work they can get away with. So even after we have increased the length of our runs steadily over several months, our leg muscles, tendons, ligaments, etc. are not prepared for the jolt that speed training delivers. The best way to stay injury-free is to gradually increase the duration and intensity. But only when we put the legs, heart, lungs, etc. to a gentle test week by week does the body respond by improving in dozens of ways.

- Mitochondria (energy powerhouse inside muscle cell) increase capacity and output.

- Mechanical efficiency of the foot is improved—more work with less effort.

- Legs go further when tired—adaptations allow you to keep going.

- Muscle cells work as a team—getting stronger, increasing performance, pumping blood back to heart.

- Mental concentration increases.

- Your spirit is unleashed as you find yourself improving.

Endorphins kill pain, making you feel good

Running at any pace, but especially speed training, signals to your body that there will be some pain to kill. The natural response is to produce natural pain killers called endorphins. These hormones act as drugs that relax and deal with muscle discomfort, while bestowing a good attitude—especially when you are tired after the run. Walking during the rest interval allows the endorphins to collect.

Gradually pushing up the workload

Your body is programmed to improve when it is gradually introduced to a little more work with enough rest afterward. Push too hard, or neglect the rest, and you'll see an increase in aches, pains and injury. When speed workouts are balanced, adjustments are made to legitimate problems and goals are realistic, most runners can continue to improve for years.

Stress + Rest = Improvement

When we run a little faster than our realistic goal pace, and increase the the number of repetitions a little more than we did on the previous speed workout, this greater workload slightly breaks down the muscle cells, tendons, etc. just enough to stimulate improvement. You see, our bodies are programmed to rebuild, to perform better than before, when slightly overwhelmed. But there must be gentle and regular stress, followed by significant rest to promote this regeneration.

Introducing the body to speed through "drills"

As a gentle introduction to faster running, I've found nothing better than the two drills that are detailed in the "Drills" chapter: Cadence Drills & Acceleration-Gliders. The former helps to improve turnover of the legs and feet. The latter provides a very gentle introduction to speedwork, in very short segments. Most of the running during the conditioning period is at an easy pace. These drills, done in the middle of a short run, once or twice a week, will improve mechanics, get the muscles ready for the heavier demands of speed training and initiate internal physiological changes in the muscles—with very little risk of injury.

A gentle increase in your weekly workouts causes a slight breakdown

The mile repeat speed workout starts with a few repetitions, with rest between each. As the number of repetitions increase with each workout, your body is pushed slightly beyond what it did before. In each workout, your muscle fibers get tired as they reach the previous maximum workload, and continue like motivated slaves to keep you running the pace assigned. In every session some are pushed beyond their capacity with each additional speed repetition. Often, pain and fatigue are not felt during the workout. But within one or two days there are usually sore muscles and tendons, and general overall tiredness. Even walking may not feel smooth for a day or two after a speed session that was run too hard.

The Damage

Looking inside the cell at the end of a hard workout, you'll see damage:

- Tears in the muscle cell membrane.

- The mitochondria (that process the energy inside the cell) are swollen.

- There's a significant lowering of the muscle stores of glycogen (the energy supply needed in speedwork).

- Waste products from exertion, bits of bone and muscle tissue and other bio junk can be found.

- Sometimes, there are small tears in the blood vessels and arteries, and blood leaks into the muscles.

The damage stimulates the muscles, tendons, etc. to rebuild stronger and better than before

Your body is programmed to get better when it is pushed beyond its current limits. A slight increase is better than a greater increase because the repair can be done relatively quickly.

You must have enough rest—if you want to rebuild stronger and better

Two days after a speed session, if the muscles have had enough rest, you'll see some improvements:

- Waste has been removed.

- Thicker cell membranes can handle more work without breaking down.

- The mitochondria have increased in size and number, so that they can process more energy next time.

- The damage to the blood system has been repaired.

- Over several months, after adapting to a continued series of small increases, more capillaries (tiny fingers of the blood system) are produced. This improves and expands the delivery of oxygen and nutrients and provides a better withdrawal of waste products.

These are only some of the many adaptations made by the incredible human body when we exercise: biomechanics, nervous system, strength, muscle efficiency and more. Internal psychological improvements occur with the physical ones. Mind, body and spirit are becoming a team, improving health and performance. An added benefit is a positive attitude.

Quality rest is crucial: 48 hours between workouts

On rest days, it's important to avoid exercises that strenuously use the calf muscles, ankle and Achilles tendon (stair machines, step aerobics, spinning out of the saddle) for the 48-hour period between running workouts. If you have other aches and pains from your individual "weak links," then don't do exercises that aggravate them further. Walking is usually a great exercise for a rest day. There are several other good exercises in the "Cross Training" section of this book. As long as you are not continuing to stress the calf, most alternative exercises are fine.

Beware of junk miles

Those training for a time goal often develop injuries because they try to "sneak in" a few miles on the days they should be resting. Even more than running long distance, speed training stresses the feet and legs and mandates the need for a 48-hour recovery period. The short, junk mile days don't help your conditioning, but they keep your muscles from recovering.

Regularity

To maintain the adaptations, you must regularly run about every 2 days. To maintain the speed improvements mentioned in this book, you should do the speed drills and mile repeats listed in the training scheduled, every week. It is OK to delay a workout every once in a while, but you need to stay on the schedule as close as possible. Missing two workouts in a row will result in a slight loss in the capacity you have been developing. The longer you wait, the harder it will be to start up again.

"Muscle memory"

Your neuromuscular system remembers the patterns of muscle activity that you have done regularly over an extended period of time. The longer you have been running regularly, the more easy it will be to start up when you've had a layoff. During your first few months of speedwork, for example, if you miss a weekly workout, you will need to drop back a week, and rebuild. But if you have run regularly for several years, and you miss a speed workout, little will be lost if you start the next one very slowly, and ease into it. Be careful as you return to speed training, if this happens.

Tip: Cramped for time? Just do a few repetitions

Let's say that you cannot get to the track on your speed day, and you don't have but 15 minutes to run. Take a 3-4 minute slow warm-up with some accelerations, and do the same, in reverse, during the last 3-5 minutes. During the middle 5-9 minutes, run several 1-2 minute accelerations at approximately the pace you would run on the track. Don't worry if the pace is not perfect. Any of these segments is better than a week without any fast running at all. Then, the following week, you can do the workout (or most of it) that had been planned this week.

Aerobic running is done during long runs

Aerobic means "in the presence of oxygen." This is the type of running you do when you feel "slow" and comfortable. When running aerobically, your muscles can get enough oxygen from the blood to process the energy in the cells (burning fat in most cases). The minimal waste products produced during aerobic running can be easily removed, with no lingering build-up in the muscles.

Speed training gets you into the anaerobic zone: producing an oxygen debt

Anaerobic running means running too fast or too long for you, on that day. At some point in the workout, when you reach your current limit, the muscles can't get enough oxygen to burn the most efficient fuel, fat. So they shift to the limited supply of stored sugar: glycogen. The waste products from this fuel pile up quickly in the cells, tightening the muscles and causing you to breathe heavily. This is called an oxygen debt. If you keep running for too long in this anaerobic state, you will have to slow down significantly or stop. But if you are running for a realistic time goal, and are pacing yourself correctly, you should only be running anaerobically for a short period of time, at the end of each workout and race.

The anaerobic threshold

As you increase the quantity of your speed sessions, you push back your anaerobic threshold. This means that you can run a bit farther than before—each workout, at the same pace, without extreme huffing and puffing. Your muscles can move your body farther and faster without going to exhaustion. Each speed workout pushes you a little bit further into the anaerobic zone. Testing yourself means running with an oxygen debt. Speed training teaches the body and mind that they can go farther before going anaerobic, how to deal with the discomfort this produces, and how to keep going when the muscles are tight and tired. It also tells you that you don't have to give up on performance when in this state. The process of coping with the stress of speedwork is the essence of running faster.

The talk test-how aerobic are you?
- You're aerobic—-if you can talk for as long as you want with minimal huffing & puffing (h & p)
- You are mostly aerobic—if you can talk for 30 sec + then must h & p for no more than 10 sec
- You are approaching anaerobic threshold—if you can only talk for 10 seconds or less, then h & p for 10+ sec
- You're anaerobic—if you can't talk more than a few words, and are mostly huffing and puffing

Fast Twitch vs. Slow Twitch Muscle Fibers

We are born with a combination of two types of muscle fibers. Those with a high percentage of fast twitchers can run fast for a short distance, and then become very tired. Fast twitch fibers are designed to burn the stored sugar in your muscles: glycogen. This is the fuel we use during the first 15 minutes of exercise (and during speedwork), and it can produce a lot of waste product, such as lactic acid. If you run even a little too fast at the beginning of a run, the muscles will become very tight and tired, very quickly, you will huff and puff, and feel increasingly uncomfortable.

If you have more slow twitch fibers, you won't be able to run as fast at first, but can keep going for longer distances. Slow twitch fibers burn fat—a fuel that is very efficient and produces little waste product. Long runs will not only condition the slow twitch fibers to work to top capacity as they efficiently burn fat. As you increase the length of the long ones, you'll train some of your fast twitch fibers to burn fat as fuel—and function as slow twitchers.

Once the starting pace is controlled (and also the ego), speed-conditioned runners develop a mix of fast and slow twitchers to do the work of running, and find that they don't get exhausted at the end. It is the slow pace and walk breaks that keep you in the aerobic (or fat-burning) zone, allowing you to push back the endurance limit.

Are you working too hard toward a time goal?
When runners get too focused on specific time goals they often feel more stress and experience some negative attitude changes. At the first sign of these symptoms, back off and let the mind and body get back together again.

- Running is not as enjoyable.
- You don't look forward to your runs.
- When you say something to others about your running, the statements are often negative.
- The negativity can permeate other areas of your life.
- You look on running as work instead of play.

The personal growth of speed training

Instead of looking just at the times in your races, embrace the life lessons that can come from the journey of an extended speed training program. Most of your runs must have some fun in them, to help you through the challenges. Even after a hard workout, focus on how good you feel afterward, and the satisfaction from overcoming adversity.

The reality of a speed training program is that you'll have more setbacks than victories. But you will learn more from the setbacks and they will make you a stronger runner—and a stronger person. Confronting challenges is initially tough, but leads you to some of the great treasure of the improvement process. As you dig for deeper resources, you find that you have more strength inside than you thought—as you discover the path to solutions that initially seemed to be too challenging for that day.

Note: There's more on this topic in the Mental Toughness chapter.

18 How Speed Training Works

The schedules in this book will gradually increase the number of mile or two mile repetitions during each workout. After each session, you'll slightly overwhelm the muscles and cardiovascular system. Your body has the incredible capacity to respond to this challenge by rebuilding stronger than before, with better efficiency.

The faster speedwork develops systems that perform at a higher capacity

Each speed segment is faster than your goal pace, by about 30 seconds per mile. The faster pace of each 2 or 1 mile repetition coaxes adaptations out of the tendons, muscles, nerve system, leg and foot mechanics. You touch lighter, use your ankle and leg muscles more efficiently, while building the strength and internal physiology to run faster.

Sustained Speed—through an increase in the number of repetitions

The maximum benefit from speed sessions is at the end of the program. As you increase the number of speed repetitions from 4 to 6, 8 and beyond, you teach yourself how to keep going at your assigned pace, even when tired. To maintain speed when tired is the mission. The only way to prepare for this "race reality" situation is to practice this during speed training. At the end of the last 3 speed sessions, you learn that you and your legs can keep performing—even when very tired. Even when tired in workouts, and the race itself, you won't tend to slow down because you've trained for this specific situation.

Longer runs maintain endurance—and improve your time

Your long runs will maintain or extend endurance, while you improve speed. Every 2-3 weeks you'll run a very slow longer run—up to 29 miles. Many runners improve their times through this long run increase as much as or more than from speed training. Both are important for maximum improvement.

Running form improves

Regular speed workouts stimulate your body to run more efficiently. On each workout, as you push into fatigue, your body intuitively searches for ways of continuing to move at the same pace without extraneous motion: lighter touch of the feet, direct foot lift, lower to the ground, quicker turnover. See the running form chapter for more details.

Watch out! Speedwork increases aches, pains and injuries

Speed training increases your chance of injury. Be sensitive to the "weak links." These are the areas on your foot, leg, muscles, etc. where you've had problems before. Think back to the patterns of aches and pains that have caused you to reduce or stop exercise in the past. You can cut injury risk significantly by taking a day or two off at the first sign of a flare-up, and by following the tips in the "troubleshooting injuries" chapter in this book.

Learn your limits. Most people go through their lives without ever testing their physical limits or experiencing the enriching experience of extending them. Once into this process, some get swept away in the quest for improvement. When runners make speed-training mistakes, they usually do too much, too soon. The series of gentle increases in the training schedules in this book will gradually extend your capacity to go further—at a slightly faster pace than you are running now. Since each person can control the effort level, you will have a chance to limit the damage. The testing process involves guessing and adjusting, going just a bit farther and then backing off. When done regularly, speed-training prepares mind, body and spirit for greater challenges.

Beware of the ego. Some of the most timid beginning runners become overly aggressive competitors. As you find your times improving through regular training, the ego tells you what you want to hear. "If you improved several minutes when following the schedule, then adding another speed session will increase the improvement." Many runners have allowed their egos to mistakenly derive all of the satisfaction from a run only if the stopwatch reads a certain time... or better. This can reduce the wonderful enjoyment of a gentle run. An ego-driven runner loses the glow of endorphins when the watch tells him/her that the time was too slow. This line of thinking often leads to slower races (due to over-training) and disappointment. Even when times are improving, if time improvement is your primary reward from running, you'll often miss the enjoyment of an achievement on the way to the next time goal. My suggestion: take time to enjoy the best part of the run—the vitality and mental attitude boost.

Performance increase is not a continuous upward trek. Be prepared to record times on at least half of your races and MMs that are slower than you think you should be running. This is often due to the ego telling you to run faster than your current ability. Be patient, learn from your setbacks, and you will generally move forward.

So take the leap of faith, and jump into the speed training program. By pushing the limits you may learn more about yourself than in any other activity in life. The real treasure is ahead: finding hidden strengths that help you get though even the toughest of tests—in races and in life itself.

19 Race Day!

After having run in races every year since 1958, I've come to believe that success comes from getting the "little things" right. As you prepare for the big day, you will be organizing yourself, gaining mental focus, reducing tension, anticipating problems as you gear up to solve them. All of this sets you up for success.

In this chapter I will cover the most crucial areas that you will need on race day. Be sure to customize the procedures based upon your needs, race venue, lifestyle, etc. Keep fine-tuning as you review. You should get more confident with each trip through the list.

Rehearsal

Use your speed workouts as "dress rehearsals" for your big day. Since you may be nervous, bring your checklists, and go through each item as you will do at the race itself. If at all possible, run on the race course several times. If this is not possible, visit the race website, study the course profile and description, and try to find venues in your area that are similar. You want to feel familiar with every aspect of the environment surrounding the venue. Success may depend upon a feeling of confidence—that you own the road on raceday.

If this is an important race that is out of town, it helps to run the course, and even stage a successful workout there. You'll learn the driving route, where to park (or which rapid transit station to exit), and what the site is like. If you will be driving, drive into the parking area several times to make sure you understand how to go exactly where you need to park. This will help you to feel at home with the staging area on race day—reducing raceday anxiety. If it's a road course, run over the last half mile of the course at least twice—the most important part of the course to know. It's also beneficial to do the first mile of the course to see which side of the road is best for walk breaks (location of sidewalks, etc.).

Rehearse your line-up position. Enter some local 5Ks, which could be run instead of the MM on those designated weekends. Practice running in the crowd, getting over to the side of the road to take walk breaks, taking water at the water stops, etc.

The afternoon before

Don't run the day before the race. You won't lose any conditioning if you take two days off from running leading up to the race. This is a personal issue and the number of days you do not run before a race is your choice. I recommend no more than two days of no running.

Some races require you to pick up your race number, and sometimes your computer chip (explained below with the day before). Look at the website or the entry form for instructions about this. A few races allow you to pick up your materials on race day—but check to be sure.

Race number

This is sometimes called a "bib number." It should be pinned on the front of the garment you'll be wearing when you cross the finish line. Ask your race organizing committee if you will have to wear a bib. If so, make sure you have 2-4 safety pins.

Computer chip

More and more races are using technology that automatically records your finish and split times along the course. You must wear a computer chip that is usually laced on the shoes, near the top. Some race result technology companies attach the chip to a velcro band around the ankle or arm. Read the instructions to make sure you are attaching this correctly. Be sure to turn this in after the race. The officials have volunteers to collect them, so stop and take them off your shoe, etc. right after the finish line. There is a steep fine ($) for those who don't turn in the chip.

The carbo loading dinner

Some races have a dinner the night before. At the dinner you will usually chat with runners at your table, and enjoy the evening. Don't eat much, however. Many runners assume, mistakenly, that they must eat a lot of food the night before. This is actually counterproductive. It takes at least 36 hours for most of the food you eat to be processed and useable in a race—usually longer. There is nothing you can eat the evening before a race that will help you.

But eating too much, or the wrong foods for you, can create a real problem. A lot of food in your gut, when you are bouncing up and down in a race, is stressful. A very common and embarrassing situation occurs when the gut is emptied to relieve this stress. While you don't want to starve yourself the afternoon and evening before, the best strategy is to eat small meals or snacks that you know are easy for the body to digest, and taper down the amount as you get closer to bed time. As always, it's best to have done a "rehearsal" of eating, so that you know what works, how much, when to stop eating, and what foods to avoid. The evening before your long morning runs is a good time to work on your eating plan so that you can replicate the successful routine leading up to raceday.

Drinking

The day before each goal race, drink about 8 glasses of water or sports drink throughout the day. If you haven't had a drink of water or sports drink in a couple of hours, drink half a cup to a cup (4-8 oz) each hour. Don't drink a lot of fluid during the morning of the race itself. This can lead to bathroom breaks before the race or the desire to do so during the race itself. Many races have porto-johns around the course, but some do not. This is another reason to preview the venue—and note the locations of bathrooms. It is a very common practice for runners that have consumed too much fluid that morning to find a tree or alley along the course. The best solution for most runners is to drink 6-10 oz of fluid about 2-3 hours before the race. Usually this is totally out of the system before the start—but practice to make sure.

Drinking Tip: If you practice drinking before your long runs, you can find the right amount of fluid that works best for you on race day. Stage your drinks so that you know when you will be taking potty breaks, comfortably before the start of the race itself—especially if you drink coffee.

The night before

Eating is optional after 5pm. If you are hungry, have a light snack (or two) that you have tested before, and has not caused problems. Less is better, but don't go to bed hungry. Continue to have about 8 oz of a good electrolyte beverage like Accelerade, about 2-3 hours before you go to bed. Avoid salty food the day before long runs and the race itself.

Alcohol is not recommended the night before, because the effects of this central nervous system depressant carry over to the next morning. Some runners have no trouble having one glass of wine or beer, while others are better off with none. In any case, alcohol will result in some dehydration—at the start of the race.

Pack your bag and lay out your clothes so that you don't have to think very much on race morning.

*   Your watch, set up for the run-walk-run ratio you are using

Note: We have timers on our website that vibrate when it's time to run, and walk.

*   A pace chart, or wrist band, with lap times, or mile times
*   Shoes
*   Socks
*   Shorts
*   Top—see clothing thermometer in this book
*   Pin race number on the front of the garment in which you will be finishing
*   A few extra safety pins for your race number, or bib number
*   Water, Accelerade, pre-race and post race beverages (such as Endurox R4), and a cooler if you wish

- Food for the drive in, and the drive home
- Bandages, skin lubricant, any other first aid items you may need
- Cash for registration if you are doing race day registration (check for exact amount, including late fee)
- $25-40 for gas, food, parking, etc.
- Race chip attached according to the race instructions
- A few jokes or stories to provide laughs or entertainment before the start
- A copy of the "race day checklist," which is just below this section

Sleep

You may sleep well, or you may not. Don't worry if you don't sleep at all. Many runners I work with every year don't sleep a wink and have the best race of their lives. Of course, don't try to go sleepless... but if it happens, don't worry.

Race Day Checklist

Photocopy this list so that you will not only have a plan, you can carry it out in a methodical way. Pack the list in your race bag. Don't try anything new the day of your race—except for health or safety issues. The only items which have been successfully used for the first time in a race are walk breaks. Even first time users benefit significantly. Otherwise, stick with your plan.

Fluid and potty stops—after you wake up, drink 4-6 oz of water every half hour. If you have used a sports drink like Accelerade about 30 minutes before your runs, prepare it. Use a cooler if you wish. In order to avoid the bathroom stops, stop your fluid intake according to the timetable of what has worked for you before. For most, this is 2 hours before.

Eat—what you have eaten before your harder runs. It is OK not to eat at all before a race unless you are a diabetic, then go with the plan that you and your doctor have worked out. Use the timetable that you have used on your long runs—follow what has worked.

Get your bearings—walk around the site to find where you want to line up, and how you will get to the start. Choose a side of the road that has more shoulder or sidewalk for ease in taking walk breaks.

Register or pick up your race number—If you already have all of your materials, you can bypass this step. If not, look at the signage in the registration area and get in the right line. Usually there is one for "race day registration" and one for those who registered online or in the mail and need to pick up their numbers.

Start your warm up 40-50 min before the start. If possible, go backwards on the course for about half a mile and turn around. This will give you a preview of the most important part of your race—the finish. Here is the warm-up routine:

- Walk for 5 minutes, slowly.
- Walk at a normal walking pace for 3-5 minutes, with a relaxed and short stride.
- Start your watch for the ratio of running and walking that you are using and do this, running and walking, for 10 minutes.
- Walk around for 5-10 minutes.
- Do 4 acceleration-gliders that gradually get you up to the speed you will be running in the race.
- Get to the staging area early and line up as far forward in your group as you can. Sit down and relax, reading your jokes or inspirational quotes. Ten minutes before the start, walk around the staging area, laugh, relax.
- Get in position and pick one side of the road or the other where you want to line up.
- When the road is closed, and runners are called onto the road, go to the curb and stay at the side of the road, near your preferred place. Visualize how you are going to start the race—comfortable and a bit conservative.

After the start
Remember that you can control how you feel during and afterward by conservative pacing and walks

- Maintain your race plan and the run/walk ratio that has worked for you—take every walk break, especially the first one.
- Be conservative in pacing for the first one-third of the race and don't let yourself be pulled out too fast on the running portions.
- Stay with your plan. As people pass you, who are running faster than you or who are not taking walk breaks, tell yourself that you will catch them later—you will!

- If anyone interprets your walking as weakness, say: "This is my proven strategy for a strong finish."
- Even if you are pushing fairly hard, enjoy the race as much as possible, smile often.
- On warm days, pour water over your head at the start, possibly wetting your running top.

Note: If the temperature is warm or other conditions prevent a top effort, slow the pace down to training pace (2 min/mi slower than goal pace or slower) and use this race as a training run. This allows you to run all-out 3-4 weeks later.

After mid-race

- When the going gets tough, do everything you can to relax, and keep the muscles resilient.
- Keep going—tell yourself this over and over during the tough moments. Shorten stride and pick up turnover.
- During the last half mile don't let your legs slow down. One more step! Success is not letting up. You can do it!

At the finish:

- In the upright position
- With a smile on your face
- Wanting to do it again

After the finish

- Keep walking for at least a quarter of a mile.
- Drink about 4-8 oz of fluid.
- Within 30 min after finishing, have a snack that is 80 % carbohydrate/20 % protein (Endurox R4 is best).
- If you can soak your legs in cool water during the first two hours after the race, do so.
- Walk for 20-30 minutes later in the day.

The next day

- Walk for 30-60 minutes, very easy. This can be done at one time, or in installments.
- Keep drinking about 4-6 oz an hour of water or sports drink like Accelerade.
- Once you qualify, register for Boston right away.

20 Mental Toughness

Bottom line:
Motivational training can give you control over your attitude. This is what makes runners mentally tough enough to keep going, when they would usually ease off.

Left Brain vs. Right Brain
The brain has two circuits that are separated and don't interconnect, which can influence our motivation. The logical left brain circuit does our business activities, trying to steer us into pleasure and away from discomfort. The creative and intuitive right circuit is an unlimited source of solutions to problems and connects us to hidden strengths.

As we accumulate stress, the left brain sends us a stream of messages telling us to "slow down," "stop and you'll feel better," "this isn't your day" and even philosophical messages like "why are you doing this?" We are all capable of staying on track, and even pushing to a higher level of performance—even when the left brain is saying these things. So the first important step in taking command over motivation is to ignore the left brain unless there is a legitimate reason of health or safety (very rare), or, in fact, you are running a lot faster than you are ready to run. You can deal with the left brain through a series of mental training drills.

Three strategies for staying mentally tough: Rehearsal, Magic Words, Dirty Tricks
These mental drills set up patterns of thinking that empower the right brain while reducing or eliminating the negative messages of the left brain. When you allow the right side of the brain to work on solutions to current problems, you increase your rate of success significantly. As the negative messages spew out of the left brain, the right brain doesn't argue. By preparing mentally for the challenges you expect, in three different ways, you will empower the right brain to deal with the problems and to develop mental toughness. Meanwhile the body gets the job done. But even more important, you will develop three strategies for success.

I. Rehearsing Success:
Rehearsals get you in the groove to perform the behaviors you need to do. In a challenging situation, you don't want to have to think about the stress or the challenge, but instead take the right action, and move from one solution to the next. The power of the rehearsal is that you have formatted your brain for a series of actions

so that you don't have to think—and the sequence becomes almost automatic. By repeating the pattern, and adjusting, you'll revise it for real life, and can become the successful runner you want to be!

Example Drill

Getting out the door early in the morning

A very common motivational problem reported to me relates to the comfort of the bed, when you wake up and know that it is time to run.

State your desired outcome: To be walking and running away from the house early in the morning.

Detail the challenge: Desire to lie in bed, no desire to exert yourself so early. The stress of the alarm clock, and having to think about what to do next when the brain isn't working very fast.

Break up the challenge into a series of actions, which lead you through the mental barriers, no one of which is challenging to the left brain.

- The night before, you're laying out running clothes and shoes, near your coffee pot, so that you don't have to think.
- Set your alarm, and say to yourself over and over: "feet on the floor, alarm off, to the coffee pot" or... "feet, alarm, coffee." As you repeat this, you visualize doing each action without thinking. By repeating it, you lull yourself to sleep. You have also been programming yourself for action the next morning.
- The alarm goes off. You shut it off, put feet on the floor, and head to the coffee pot—all without thinking.
- You're putting on one piece of clothing at a time, sipping coffee, never thinking about running.
- With coffee cup in hand, you walk out the door to see what the weather is like.
- Sipping coffee, you walk to the edge of your block or property to see what the neighbors are doing.
- Putting coffee down, you cross the street, and you have made the break!
- The endorphins are kicking in, you feel good, you want to continue.

Performance Drill
Pushing past the fatigue point when you tend to slow down

You're into a hard workout or race, and you are really tired. Your left brain is telling you that you can't reach your goal today, "just slow down a little, there are other days to work hard."

Evaluate whether there is a real medical reason why you can't run as projected. If there is a reason, back off and conserve—there will be another day.

Almost every time, however, the problem is more simple: you are not willing to push through the discomfort. The most effective way of getting tough mentally is to gradually push back your limits. Speed training programs can help you greatly. As you add to the number of repetitions each workout, you'll work on the mind as the body gets all systems working together to run faster.

Don't quit! Mental toughness can be as simple as not giving up. Just ignore the negative messages, and stay focused to the finish. If you've trained adequately, hang on and keep going.

In your speed workouts, practice the following drill. Fine-tune this so that when you run your goal race, you will have a strategy for staying mentally tough.

The scene:
You're getting very tired, you'd really like to call it quits, or at least slow down significantly.

Quick strategies:
Break up the remaining workout or race into segments that you know you can do:
*   "1 more minute." Run for one minute, then reduce pace slightly for 10 seconds, then say "1 more minute" again, and again.
*   "10 more steps." Run about 10 steps, take a couple of easy steps, then say "ten more steps."
*   "One more step." Keep saying this over and over—you'll get there.

Take some shuffle breaks

- Reduce the tension on your leg muscles and feet by shuffling for a few strides every 1-2 minutes. By practicing "the shuffle," you'll find that you don't slow down much at all—while your muscles feel better.

Mile by mile

- In the speed workouts, start each lap saying to yourself—"just one more" (even if you have 4 to go) or "I'll just run half a lap." You'll run the whole thing in most cases.

- When you are getting close to the end and really feel like you can't keep going, say to yourself "I am tough" or "I can endure" or "Yes I can."

II. Magic Words

Even the most motivated person has sections of a tough workout or race when he or she wants to quit. By using a successful brainwashing technique, you can pull yourself through these negative thoughts, and feel like a champion at the end. On these days you have not only crossed the finish line—you've overcome challenges to get there.

Think back to the problems that you face in your tough workouts or races. These are the ones that are most likely to challenge you again. As you go through a series of speed sessions and long runs, you will encounter just about every problem you will face. Go back in your memory bank and pull out instances when you started to lose motivation due to these, but finished and overcame the challenge.

Relax...Power...Glide

In really tough runs, I have three challenges that occur over and over: 1) I become tense when I get really tired, worried that I will struggle badly at the end. 2) I feel the loss of the bounce and strength I had at the beginning, and worry that there will be no strength at the end. 3) My form starts to get ragged and I worry about further deterioration of muscles and tendons and more fatigue due to "wobbling."

Over the past four decades I have learned to counter these three problems with the magic words "Relax...Power...Glide." The visualization of each of these positives helps a little. The real magic comes from the association I have made with hundreds of successful experiences when I started to "lose it" in one of the three areas, but overcame the problems. Each time I "run through" one or more of the problems, I associate the experience with these magic words and add to the magic.

Now, when something starts to go wrong, I repeat the three words, over and over. Instead of increasing my anxiety, the repetition of the words calms me down. Even though I don't feel as strong at mile 21 as I did at mile one, I'm empowered just by knowing that I have a strategy and can draw upon my past experience. And when my legs lose the bounce, I make adjustments and keep going.

When I say magic words that are associated with successful experience, there are two positive effects. The saying of the words floods the brain with positive memories. For a while, the negative messages of the left brain don't have a chance and I can get down the road for a mile or two. But the second effect may be more powerful. The words directly link you to the right brain, which works intuitively to make the same connections that allowed you solve the problems before.

To be successful on any day, don't give up. Most of the time, you can get through the "bad parts" by not making adjustments, putting one foot in front of the other. If the body has done all of the training in this book, the weather is appropriate for your goal, and you are mentally prepared, you will push beyond the negative left brain messages during a series of workouts and earlier races. This develops the confidence to do it again, and again. Feel free to use my magic words, or develop your own. The more experiences you have associated with the words, the more magic they have.

III. Dirty Tricks
The strategy of the rehearsal drill will get you focused and organized, while reducing the stress of the first section of the race. Magic words will pull you through most of the challenging parts. But on the really rough days, it helps to have some tricks to play on the left side of the brain.

"Dirty Tricks" are quick fixes that distract the left brain for a while, allowing you to get down the road. These imaginative and sometimes crazy images may not have any logic behind them. But when you counter a left brain message with a creative idea, you often confuse the left brain and stop the flow of negative messages.

The giant invisible rubber band

When I get tired on long or hard runs, I unpack this secret weapon, and throw it around someone ahead of me—or someone who had the audacity to pass me. For a while, the person doesn't realize that he or she has been "looped" and continues to push onward while I get the benefit of being pulled along. After a minute or two of mentally projecting myself into this image, I have to laugh for believing in such an absurd notion. But laughing activates the creative right side of the brain. This usually generates several more entertaining ideas, especially when done on a regular basis.

The right brain has millions of dirty tricks. Once you get it activated, you are likely to experience its solutions to problems you are currently having. It can entertain you as you get closer to your finish, step-by-step.

For many more dirty tricks and mental strategies, see **Galloway's Book on Running Second Edition** and **Marathon—You Can Do It**.

21 Cross Training: Getting Better as You Rest the Legs

The best item you can insert into a speed training program to reduce injury is an extra rest day or two. The hard work of running involves lifting your body off the ground, and then absorbing the shock. If you are doing this every other day—even when doing speedwork, you'll limit the damage that is usually repaired. Many runners, especially those in their 40's, 50's and 60's, don't have injury layoffs when running every other day.

Once runners get into a speed program, and start to improve, some will try to sneak in an extra day or two on the days that should be "off." They often feel, mistakenly, that they can gain performance with an additional day; or that they are losing fitness when they take a day off. This perception does not match up with reality. Even with easy and short runs (on days that should be off) the legs cannot fully recover—especially from speed workouts. These short runs on rest days give you the so-called "junk miles" which increase fatigue and injury risk.

Cross Training Activities

The middle ground is to run one day, and cross-train the next. Cross training simply means "alternative exercise" to running. Your goal is to find exercises that give you a good feeling of exertion, but do not fatigue the workhorses of running: calf muscles, Achilles tendon, feet.

The other exercises may not deliver the same good feelings as running—but they can come close. Many runners report that it may take a combination of 3 or 4 segments in a session to do this. But even if you don't feel exactly the same way, you'll receive the relaxation that comes from exercise, while you burn calories and fat.

EASE INTO A NEW EXERCISE!

1. Start with 5 easy minutes of exercise, rest for 20 or more minutes and do 5 more easy minutes.

2. Take a day of rest between this exercise (you can do a different exercise the next day).

3. Increase by 2-3 additional minutes each session until you get to the number of minutes that gives you the appropriate feeling of exertion.

4. Once you can do two 15 minute sessions, you could shift to one 22-25 minute session and increase by 2-3 more minutes per session if you wish.

5. It's best to do no exercise the day before a long run, a very hard speed session, or a race.

6. To maintain your conditioning in each alternative exercise, do one session each week of 10 minutes or more once you reach that amount. If you have the time, you can cross-train (XT) on all of your days off from running—except listed in #5 above.

7. The maximum cross training is up to the individual. As long as you are feeling fine for the rest of the day and having no trouble with your runs the next day, the length of your cross training should not be a problem.

Water running can improve your running form

All of us have little flips and side motions of our legs that interfere with our running efficiency. During a water running workout, the resistance of the water forces your legs to find a more efficient path. In addition, several leg muscles are strengthened which can help to keep your legs on a smoother path when they get tired at the end of a long run.

Here's how!

You'll need a flotation belt for this exercise. The product "aqua jogger" is designed to float you off the bottom of the pool, and on most runners, tightens so that it is close to the body. There are many other ways to keep you floating, including water ski float belts and life jackets.

Get in the deep end of the pool and move your legs through a running motion. This means little or no knee lift, kicking out slightly in front of you, and bringing the leg behind, with the foot coming up behind you. As in running, your lower leg should be parallel with the horizontal during the back-kick.

If you are not feeling much exertion, you're probably lifting the knees too high and moving your legs through a small range of motion. To get the benefit, an extended running motion is needed.

It's important to do water running once a week to keep the adaptations that you have gained. If you miss a week, you should drop back a few minutes from your previous session. If you miss more than 3 weeks, start back at two 5-8 min sessions.

Fat burning and overall fitness exercises

Nordic Track

This exercise machine simulates the motion used in cross country skiing. It is one of the better cross training modes for fat burning because it uses a large number of muscle cells while raising body temperature. If you exercise at an easy pace, you can get into the fat burning zone (past 45 minutes) after a gradual build up to that amount. This exercise requires no pounding of the legs or feet and (unless you push it too hard or too long) allows you to run as usual the next day.

Rowing Machine

There are a number of different types of rowing machines. Some work the legs a bit too hard for runners, but most allow you to use a wide variety of lower and upper body muscle groups. Like Nordic track, if you have the right machine for you, it's possible to continue to exercise for about as long as you wish, once you have gradually worked up to this. Most of the better machines are good fat-burners: they use a large number of muscle cells, raise temperature, and can be continued for more than three-quarters of an hour.

Cycling

Indoor cycling (on an exercise cycle) is a better fat burner exercise than outdoor cycling, because it raises your body temperature more—you don't get the cooling effect of the breeze that you generate on a bike. The muscles used in both indoor and outdoor cycling are mostly the quadraceps muscles—on the front of the thigh—reducing the total number of muscle cells compared with water running, nordic track, etc.

Elliptical

Because you don't use the calf muscles on this machine, it can be used on a non-running day. While this will not improve your running performance, it can give you a good cardiovascular workout, on a day when you can't run for some reason.

Don't forget walking!

Walking can be done all day long. I call walking a "stealth fat-burner" exercise because it is so easy to walk mile after mile—especially in small doses. But it is also an excellent cross training exercise—this includes walking on the treadmill. Caution: Don't walk with a long stride.

Cross Training for the upper body

Weight training

While weight work is not a great fat-burning exercise, and does not directly benefit running, it can be done on non-running days, or on running days, after a run. There are a wide range of different ways to build strength. If interested, find a coach that can help you build strength in the muscle groups you wish to be strengthened. As mentioned previously in this book, weight training for the legs is not recommended.

Note: I do two exercises that have helped me maintain the strength of my postural muscles.

The Crunch—lie on your back, on carpet or any padded surface. Lift your head and upper back slightly off the floor. Go through a narrow range of motion so that you feel your abdominal muscles contracting almost constantly. Start with a few seconds of these, and build up to 30-60 seconds, done 3-5 times a day (one or two days a week)

Arm running—while standing, with hand held weights (milk jugs, etc.) move your arms through a wide range of motion you would use when running—maybe slightly more than usual. Keep the weights close to the body. Start with a few reps, and gradually build up to 3-5 sets of 10. Pick a weight that is challenging enough so that you feel exertion at the end of a set of 10. You don't want to have to struggle during the last few reps.

Swimming

While not a fat-burner, swimming strengthens the upper body, while improving cardiovascular fitness and endurance in those muscles. Swimming can be done on both running days and non-running days.

Push-ups and Pull-ups

These can build great upper body strength as you innovate to work the upper body muscle groups you want to strengthen. If interested, see a strength expert for these variations.

Don't Do These on Non-Running Days!

The following exercises will tire the muscles used for running and keep them from recovering between run days. If you really like to do any of these exercises, you can do them after a run, on a short running day.

- Stair machines
- Stair aerobics
- Weight training for the leg muscles
- Power walking—especially on a hilly course
- Spinning classes (on a bicycle) in which you stand up on the pedals and push

22 Dealing with the Heat

"Forget about a personal record when it's over 60F"

If you slow down a little on a warm day, you can finish strong, with a higher finish place. That seems obvious, but some runners "lose it" at the beginning of a hot race. The result is a much slower time—because of the inevitable slowdown at the end. For every second you run too fast during the first mile of a race on a hot day, you can usually expect to run 5-10 seconds slower at the end.

When you exercise strenuously in even moderate heat (above 60F), you raise core body temperature. Most beginning runners will see the internal temperature rise above 55F. This triggers a release of blood into the capillaries of your skin to help cool you down. This diversion reduces the blood supply available to your exercising muscles, meaning that you will have less blood and less oxygen delivered to the power source that moves you forward—and less blood to move out the waste products from these work sites. As the waste builds up in the muscle, you will slow down.

So the bad news is that in warm weather you are going to feel worse and run slower. The worse news is that working too hard on a hot day could result in a very serious condition called heat disease. Make sure that you read the section on this health problem at the end of this chapter. You can adapt to these conditions to some extent, as you learn the best time of the day, clothing, and other tricks to keep you cool. But it is always better to back off or stop running at the first sign that you may be coming into this condition. The following are proven ways of avoiding heat adversity.

Running the long workouts during summer heat

1. Run before the sun gets above the horizon. Get up early during the warm months and you will avoid most of the dramatic stress from the sun. This is particularly a problem in humid areas. Early morning is usually the coolest time of the day. Without having to deal with the sun, most runners can gradually adapt to heat. At the very least, your runs will be more enjoyable than later in the day.

Note: Be sure to take care of safety issues.

2. If you must run when the sun is up, pick a shady course. Shade provides a significant relief in areas of low humidity, and some relief in humid environments.

3. In areas of low humidity, it's usually cool during the evening and night. In humid environments there may not be much relief. The coolest time of the day when it's humid is usually just before dawn.

4. Have an indoor facility available. With treadmills, you can exercise in air conditioning. If a treadmill bores you, alternate segments of 5-10 minutes—one segment outdoors, and the next indoors.

5. Don't wear a hat! You lose most of your body heat through the top of your head. Covering the head will cause a quicker internal buildup of heat.

6. Wear light clothing, but not cotton. Many of the new, technical fibers (Dry Science, Polypro, Coolmax, Dri-Fit, etc.) will move moisture away from your skin, producing a cooling effect. Cotton soaks up the sweat, making the garment heavier as it sticks to your skin. This means that you won't receive as much of a cooling effect as that provided by the tech products.

7. Pour water over your head. Evaporation not only helps the cooling process—it makes you feel cooler. This offers a psychological boost which can be huge. If you can bring along ice water with you, you will feel a lot cooler as you squirt some regularly over the top of your head—using a pop top water bottle.

8. Do your short runs in installments. It is fine, on a hot day that is scheduled for an easy run, to put in your 30 minutes by doing 10 in the morning, 10 at noon and 10 at night. The long run, however, should be done at one time. Speed workouts should also be done all at once, but you may take more rest between speed reps, and you may break up the distance when it's hot (running twice as many 800's as one mile repeats).

9. Take a pool break, or a shower chill-down. During a run, it really helps to take a 2-4 minute dip in a pool or a shower. Some runners in hot areas run loops around their neighborhood and let the hose run over the head each lap. The pool is especially helpful in soaking out excess body temperature. I have run in 97 degree temperatures at our Florida running retreat, breaking up a 5 mile run into 3 x 1.7 mi. Between each, I take a 2-3 minute "soak break" and get back out there. It was only at the end of each segment that I got warm again.

10. Sunscreen—a mixed review. Some runners will need to protect themselves. Some products, however, produce a coating on the skin, slowing down the perspiration and producing an increase in body temperature build-up. If you are only in the sun for 30-50 minutes at a time, you may not need to put on sunscreen for cancer protection. Consult with a dermatologist for your specific needs—or find a product that doesn't block the pores.

11. When you are not running, drink 6-8 oz of a sports drink like Accelerade or water at least every 2 hours, or when thirsty, throughout the day during hot weather.

12. Look at the clothing thermometer at the end of this section. Wear loose fitting garments that have some texture in the fabric. Texture will limit or prevent the perspiration from causing a clinging and sticking to the skin.

13. When the temperature is above 90F, you have my permission to re-arrange your running shoes—preferably in an air-conditioned environment.

Here's How to Adjust the Pace of Long Runs—And the Marathon

As the temperature rises above 55F, your body starts to build up heat, but most runners aren't significantly slowed until 60F. If you make the adjustments early, you won't have to suffer later and slow down a lot more at that time. The baseline for this table is 60F or 14C.

Between 60F and 64F—slow down 30 seconds per mile slower than you would run at 60F

Between 14C and 16.5C, slow down 20 seconds per kilometer than you would run at 14C

Between 65F and 69F—Slow down one minute per mile slower than you would run at 60F

Between 17C and 19.5C—slow down 40 seconds per kilometer slower than you would run at 14C

Between 70F and 74F—slow down 1:30/mile slower than you would run at 60F

Between 20C and 22C—slow down one minute/kilometer slower than you would run at 14C

Between 75F and 79F—slow down 2 min/mi slower than you would run at 60F

Between 22.5C and 25C—slow down 1:20/km slower than you would run at 14C

Above 80F and 25C—be careful, take extra precautions to avoid heat disease

Or... exercise indoors

Or... arrange your shoes next to the air conditioner

Heat Disease Alert!

While it is unlikely that you will push yourself into heat disease, the longer you are exercising in hot (and/or humid) conditions, the more you increase the likelihood of experiencing this dangerous medical situation. That's why I recommend breaking up your exercise into short segments when it's hot, if you must run outdoors. Be sensitive to your reactions to the heat, and those of the runners around you. When one of the symptoms is present, this is normally not a major problem unless there is significant distress. But when several are experienced, take action because heat disease can lead to death. It's always better to be conservative: stop the workout and cool off.

Symptoms:

- Intense heat build-up in the head
- General overheating of the body
- Significant headache
- Significant nausea
- General confusion and loss of concentration
- Loss of muscle control
- Excessive sweating and then cessation of sweating
- Clammy skin
- Excessively rapid breathing
- Muscle cramps
- Feeling faint
- Unusual heart beat or rhythm

Risk factors:

- Viral or bacterial infection
- Taking medication—especially cold medicines, diruretics, medicines for diarrhea, antihistamines, atropine, scopolamine, tranquilizers, even cholesterol and blood pressure medications. Check with your doctor on medication issues—especially when running in hot weather.
- Dehydration (especially due to alcohol)
- Severe sunburn
- Overweight
- Lack of heat training
- Exercising more than one is used to
- Occurrence of heat disease in the past

- Two or more nights of extreme sleep deprivation
- Certain medical conditions including high cholesterol, high blood pressure, extreme stress, asthma, diabetes, epilepsy, cardiovascular disease, smoking, or a general lack of fitness
- Drug use, including alcohol, over-the-counter medications, prescription drugs, etc. (Consult with your doctor about using drugs when you are exercising hard in hot weather.)

Take action! Call 911

Use your best judgment, but in most cases anyone who exhibits two or more of the symptoms should get into a cool environment, and get medical attention immediately. An extremely effective cool off method is to soak towels, sheets or clothing in cool or cold water, and wrap them around the individual. If ice is available, sprinkle some ice over the wet cloth.

Heat adaptation workout

If you regularly force yourself to deal with body heat buildup, your body will get better at running closer to your potential when hot. As with all training components, it is important to do this regularly. You should be sweating to some extent at the end of the workout, although the amount and the duration of perspiration is an individual issue. If the heat is particularly difficult, cut back the amount. Don't let yourself get into the beginning stages of heat disease. Get doctor's clearance before doing this.

Important Note: Read the section on heat disease and stop your workout if you sense that you are even beginning to become nauseous, lose concentration or mental awareness of your condition, etc.

- Done on a short running day once a week.
- Do the run-walk ratio that you usually use, going at a very easy pace.
- Warm up with a 5 min walk and take a 5 min walk warm-down.
- Temperature should be between 75F and 85F (22-27C) for best results.
- Stop at the first sign of nausea or significant heat stress, or other symptoms of heat disease.
- When less than 70F (19C), you can put on additional layers of clothing to simulate a higher temperature.
- First session, run-walk for only 8-10 minutes in the heat.
- Each successive session, add 2-3 minutes.

- Build up to a maximum of 25 minutes—but don't push into heat disease.
- Regularity is important to maintain adaptations—once every week.
- If you miss a week or more, reduce the amount significantly and rebuild.

Tip: Maintaining heat tolerance during the winter

By putting on additional layers of clothing so that you sweat within 3-4 minutes of your run-walk, you can keep much of your summer heat conditioning—that took so much work to produce. Continue to run for a total of 12-20 minutes or more as you build according to the sidebar above.

23. Choosing the Best Shoe for You

If you have a good technical running store in your area, go there to get help in fitting. The advice you can receive from experienced shoe fitters will be priceless. My store, Phidippides, has some information on the website **www.Phidippides.com**. Here are some other helpful tips:

1. Look at the wear pattern on your most worn pair of walking or running shoes. Use the guide below to help you choose about 3 pairs of shoes from one of the categories below:

Flexible?
If you have the wear pattern of a "floppy" or flexible foot, on the inside of the forefoot, and have some foot or knee pain, look at a neutral shoe that does not have a lot of cushion in the forefoot.

Flexible—Overpronated Foot?

The wear pattern shows significant wear on the inside of the forefoot. If there is knee or hip pain, look for a shoe that has "structure" or anti-pronation capabilities. If you don't have pain, look at a neutral shoe that does not have a lot of cushion in the forefoot.

Rigid?

If you have a wear pattern on the outside of the forefoot of the shoe, and no wear on the inside, you probably have a rigid foot, and can choose a neutral shoe that has adequate cushion and flexibility for you, as you run and walk in them.

Can't tell?

Choose shoes that are neutral or mid range of cushion and support.

- Set aside at least 30 minutes to choose your next shoe.
- Run and walk, on a pavement surface, to compare the shoes. If you have a floppy foot, make sure that you get the support you need.
- You want a shoe that feels natural on your foot—no pressure or aggravation—while allowing the foot to go through the range of motion needed for running.
- Again, take as much time as you need before deciding.
- If the store doesn't let you run in the shoe, go to another store.

2. Go by fit and not the size noted on the box of the shoe.

    Most runners wear a running shoe that is about 2 sizes larger than their street shoe. For example, I wear a size 10 street shoe but run in a size 12 running model. Be open to getting the best fit—regardless of what size you see on the running shoe box.

3. Include extra room for your toes.

    Your foot tends to swell during the day, so it's best to fit your shoes after noontime. Be sure to stand up in the shoe during the fitting process to measure how much extra room you have in the toe region of the shoe. Pay attention to the longest of your feet, and leave at least half an inch.

On Race Day: Racing shoe or lightweight training shoe?

Most of the high performance racing shoes will lose their cushioning and bounce by the 20-mile mark in a marathon. Most of the runners I've followed who have tried both types of shoes have had better success with a lightweight training shoe. Start breaking in your race shoe about 2 months prior to race day, by wearing them one day a week for 2 miles on an easy run. It's also recommended that you wear them during 3-4 mile repeats, during your last two mile repeat workouts.

Width issues

*   Running shoes tend to be a bit wider than street shoes.
*   Usually, the lacing can "snug up" the difference, if your foot is a bit narrower.
*   The shoe shouldn't be laced too tight around your foot because the foot swells during running and walking. On hot days, the average runner will move up one-half shoe size.
*   In general, running shoes are designed to handle a certain amount of "looseness." But if you are getting blisters when wearing a loose shoe, tighten the laces.
*   Several shoe companies have some shoes in different widths.
*   The shoe is too narrow if you are rolling off the edge of the shoe as you push off—on either side.

Shoes for women

Women's shoes tend to be slightly narrower than those for men, and the heel is usually a bit smaller. The quality of the major running shoe brands is equal whether for men or women. But about 25 % of women runners have feet that can fit better into men's shoes. Usually the confusion comes when women wear large sizes. The better running stores can help you make a choice in this area.

Breaking in a new shoe

- Wear the new shoe around the house, for an hour or more each day for a week. If you stay on carpet, and the shoe doesn't fit correctly, you can exchange it at the store. But if you have put some wear on the shoe, dirt, etc., few stores will take it back.

- In most cases you will find that the shoe feels comfortable enough to run immediately. It is best to continue walking in the shoe, gradually allowing the foot to accommodate to the arch, the heel, the ankle pads, and to make other adjustments. If you run in the shoe too soon, blisters are often the result.

- If there are no rubbing issues on the foot when walking, you could walk in the new shoe for a gradually increasing amount, for 2-4 days.

- On the first run, just run about half a mile in the shoe. Put on your old shoes and continue the run.

- On each successive run, increase the distance run in the new shoe for 3-4 runs. At this point, you will usually have the new shoe broken in.

How do you know when it's time to get a new shoe?

1. When you have been using a shoe for 3-4 weeks successfully, buy another pair of exactly the same model, make, size, etc. The reason for this: The shoe companies often make significant changes or discontinue shoe models (even successful ones) every 6-8 months.

2. Walk around the house in the new shoe for a few days.

3. After the shoe feels broken in, run the first half-mile of one of your weekly runs in the new shoe, then put on the shoe that is already broken in.

4. On the "shoe break-in" day, gradually run a little more in the new shoe. Continue to do this only one day a week.

5. Several weeks later you will notice that the new shoe offers more bounce than the old one.

6. When the old shoe doesn't offer the support you need, shift to the new pair.

7. Start breaking in a third pair.

24 The Clothing Thermometer

What to wear, based upon the temperature

After years of working with people in various climates, here are my recommendations for the appropriate clothing based upon the temperature. First, choose garments that will be comfortable—especially next to your skin, and especially at the end of a run. You may have to resist the temptation to buy a fashion color, but function is most important. Watch for seams and bunching up in areas where you will have body parts rubbing together, thousands of times during a run.

Cotton is usually not a good fabric for those who perspire a great deal. The cotton will absorb the sweat, hold it next to your skin, and increase the weight you must carry during the run. Garments made out of fabric labeled Dry Science, Polypro, Coolmax, Dri-Fit, etc., hold enough body heat close to you in winter, while releasing extra heat. In summer and winter, they move moisture away from the skin—cooling you in hot weather, and avoiding a chill in the winter—and limiting the weight increase from perspiration.

Note: Mizuno has a new technology called "breath thermo" that heats up when you start to perspire. This is great for cold weather as you may use a much lighter garment that keeps you warm.

Temperature	What to wear
14C or 60F	and above Tank top or singlet, and shorts
9 to13C or 50 to 59F	T-shirt and shorts
5 to 8C or 40 to 49F	Long sleeve lightweight shirt, shorts or tights (or nylon long pants) Mittens and gloves
0 to 4C or 30 to 39F	Long sleeve medium weight shirt, and another T-shirt, tights and shorts, Socks or mittens or gloves and a hat over the ears
-4 to −1C or 20-29F	Medium weight long sleeve shirt, another T shirt, tights and shorts, socks, mittens or gloves, and a hat over the ears
-8 to −3C or 10-19F	Medium weight long sleeve shirt, and medium/heavy weight shirt, Tights and shorts, nylon wind suit, top and pants, socks, thick mittens and a hat over the ears

-12 to −7C or 0-9F	Two medium or heavyweight long sleeve tops, thick tights, Thick underwear (especially for men), Medium to heavy warm up, Gloves and thick mittens, ski mask, a hat over the ears, and Vaseline covering any exposed skin.
-18 to −11C or −15F	Two heavyweight long sleeve tops, tights and thick tights, thick underwear (and supporter for men), thick warm up (top and pants) mittens over gloves, thick ski mask and a hat over ears, vasoline covering any exposed skin, thicker socks on your feet and other foot protection, as needed.

Minus 20 both C & F Add layers as needed

What not to wear

1. A heavy coat in winter. If the layer is too thick, you'll heat up, sweat excessively, and cool too much when you take it off.
2. No shirt for men in summer. Fabric that holds some of the moisture will give you more of a cooling effect as you run.
3. Too much sunscreen—it can interfere with sweating.
4. Socks that are too thick in summer. Your feet swell and the pressure from the   socks can increase the chance of a black toenail and blisters.
5. Lime green shirt with bright pink polka dots (unless you have a lot of confidence and/or can run fast).

Special cases:

Chaffing can be reduced by lycra and other fabric. Many runners have eliminated chaffing between the legs by using a lycra "bike tight" as an undergarment. These are also called "lycra shorts." There are several skin lubricants on the market, including Glide.

Male nipple irritation Some men suffer from irritation of their nipples. Having a slick and smooth fabric across the chest will reduce this. There is now a product called Nip-Guard that has allowed many men to completely avoid the problem.

25 Practical Eating Issues

Most of the nutritional problems that I hear about are due to eating too much, ingesting too soon before running or consuming the wrong foods. While there are many individual differences in all of the eating variables, it's always better to err on the side of eating less—the closer you get to the workout or race.

Practical eating issues

- You don't need to eat before a run, unless your blood sugar is low. In this case,

the best situation is to eat a snack that has never caused digestive problems within 30 minute before the start.

- Reload most effectively by eating (100-300 calories) within 30 min of the finish of a run (80 % carb/20 % protein). Avoid fat within 90 minutes of the finish of a hard run.

- Eating or drinking too much right before the start of a run will interfere with deep breathing, & may cause side pain. The food or fluid in your stomach limits your intake of air into the lower lungs, and restricts the diaphragm—causing pain in the area just below the ribs.

- If you are running low on blood sugar at the end of your long runs or long workouts, take some blood sugar booster with you (gel-type products). The rule of thumb is to consume 30-40 calories, every 1-2 miles, after mile # 4-6. Test this during long runs and find the pattern that works for you.

- It is never a good idea to eat a huge meal. Those who claim that they must "carbo load" are often rationalizing the desire to eat a lot of food. Eating a big meal the night before (or the day of) a race, or before a hard workout or a long run can be a real problem. The food will require an extensive blood flow to the gut, depriving the exercising muscles of this precious fluid. In addition, you will have a lot of food in your gut, as you bounce up and down for an extended period. This could get ugly.

- A radical change in the foods you eat is not a good idea, and usually leads to problems—especially within 12 hours before a hard workout or race.

The bad side of fat

There are two kinds of fat that have been found to cause narrowing of the arteries around the heart and leading to your brain: saturated fat and trans fat. Mono and unsaturated fats, from vegetable sources, are often healthy—olive oil, nuts, avocado and safflower oil. Some fish oils have Omega 3 fatty acids, which have been shown to have a protective effect on the heart. Some fish, however, have oil that is not protective.

Look carefully at the labels because a lot of foods have vegetable oils that have been processed into trans fat. A wide range of baked goods and other foods have this unhealthy substance. Since labels are often confusing, call the 800 number to check on the kind of fat in this case. Your other choice is to avoid the food.

When to watch water intake

It is important to drink regularly. But during extremely long runs of over 4 hours, medical experts from major marathons recommend no more than 20 oz an hour of fluid. Most folks need less than this. For most runners, this means drinking about 4 oz (half a glass) every 1-2 miles.

Sweat the electrolytes

Electrolytes are the salts that your body loses when you sweat: sodium, potassium, magnesium and calcium. When you have not restocked your supply of these, your fluid transfer system doesn't work as well and you may experience ineffective cooling, muscle cramps (see the next chapter), and other problems. Most runners have no problem replacing these in a normal diet, but if you are experiencing cramping during or after exercise, regularly, you may be low in sodium or potassium. The best product I've found for replacing these minerals is called SUCCEED. If you have high blood pressure, a mineral imbalance, etc., get your doctor's guidance before taking any salt supplement.

When you are sweating a lot, it is a good idea to drink 2-3 glasses a day of a good electrolyte beverage.

Drinking/eating schedule before a hard morning run

Note: Test this in training to find the strategy that works for you.

- 1 hour before a morning run: either a cup of coffee or a glass of water. If you need to eat something, have half of an energy bar or a packet of a gel-type product.
- 30 min before any run (if blood sugar is low and you have not had any food) approx. 100 calories of a drink that has 80 % carbohydrate and 20 % protein (or 100 % carbohydrate if you cannot find the 20 % protein drinks).
- Within 30 min after a run: approx. 200 calories of a 80 % carb/20 % protein snack (Endurox R4, for example).
- If you are sweating a lot during hot weather, 3-4 glasses of a good electrolyte beverage like Accelerade, throughout the day, when you are not running.

Get insulin working for you

For best results in raising blood sugar when it is too low (within 30 minutes before a run) a snack should have about 80 % of the calories in simple carbohydrate and 20 % in protein. This promotes the production of insulin, which is helpful before a run in processing the carbohydrate into a form (glycogen) that the muscles can use very quickly. The product Accelerade has worked best among the thousands of runners I hear from every year. It has the 80 %/20 % ratio of carb to protein. If you eat an energy bar with the 80/20 ratio, be sure to drink 6-8 oz of water or coffee with it. Many runners consume an energy bar (or half an energy bar) about an hour before exercise. Experts recommend drinking less than 20 oz an hour during a long run.

Eating during exercise

Most exercisers don't need to worry about eating or drinking during a run of less than 90 minutes. In fact, the body shuts down in its ability to process almost anything, and eating even sports nutrition products can make you nauseous. But when your slow long runs exceed 90 minutes, the blood sugar level starts to drop. At this point, there are several options listed below. Most runners find it productive to start taking the food product about 50-60 minutes into the workout. This helps when running long, or during a long speed session. The general rule of thumb is 30-40 calories, every 1-2 miles.

Gel-type products—these come in small packets, and are the consistency of honey or thick syrup. The most successful way to take them is to put the contents of 1-2 packets in a small plastic bottle with a pop-top. About every 10-15 minutes, take a small squirt with a sip or two of water.

Energy Bars—Cut into 8-10 pieces and take a piece, with a couple of sips of water, every 10-15 minutes.

Candy—particularly gummi bears or hard candies. The usual consumption is 1-2 pieces, about every 10 minutes.

Sports Drinks—Since nausea is experienced by a significant number of those who drink these products during exercise, I'm not going to recommend these during a run. If you have had success when using sports drinks in workouts or races, drink it in the same quantity and on the same schedule as you have used it before.

Exception: During your rest interval, when doing speed repetitions, a slightly diluted sports drink like Accelerade has helped maintain BSL and speeded recovery, according to research.

It is important to re-load after exercise—within 30 minutes

Whenever you have finished a hard or long workout (for you), a reloading snack of about 200-300 calories will help you recover faster. Again, the 80/20 ratio of carb to protein has been most successful in replenishing the glycogen stores into the muscle cells. The product that has worked best for the thousands of runners I work with each year is Endurox R4.

26 Troubleshooting Performance

Times are slowing down at end
- Your long runs aren't long enough.
- You are running too fast at the beginning of the race.
- You may benefit from walk breaks that are taken more frequently.
- You may be overtrained—back off the speed sessions for a week or two.
- In track workouts, run hardest at the end of the workout.
- Temperature and/or humidity may be to blame—try slowing down at the beginning.

Slowing down in the middle of the race
- You may be running too hard at the beginning—slow down by a few seconds each mile.
- You may benefit from more frequent walk breaks.
- In track workouts, work the hardest in the middle of the workout.

Nauseous at the end
- You ran too fast at the beginning or the middle.
- Temperature is above 65F/17C.
- You ate too much (or drank too much) before the race or workout—even hours before.
- You ate the wrong foods—most commonly fatty fried foods, milk products, fibrous foods.

Tired during workouts
- Low in B vitamins
- Low in iron—have a serum ferritin test
- Not eating enough protein
- Blood sugar is low before exercise
- Not eating within 30 min of the finish of a run
- Eating too much fat—especially before or right after a run
- Running too many days per week
- Running too hard on long runs
- Running too hard on all running days
- Not taking enough walk breaks from the beginning of your runs
- Insufficient rest days between hard workouts

27 Problems/Solutions

Side Pain

This is very common, and usually has a simple fix. Normally it is nothing to worry about... it just hurts. This condition is due to 1) the lack of lower lung breathing, and 2) going a little too fast from the beginning of the run. You can correct #2 easily by slowing your pace during the first mile or two.

Lower lung breathing from the beginning of a run can prevent side pain. This way of inhaling air is performed by diverting the air you breathe into your lower lungs. Also called "belly breathing," this is how we breathe when asleep, and it provides maximum opportunity for oxygen absorption. If you don't breathe this way when you run, and you are not getting the oxygen you need, the side pain will tell you. By slowing down, walking and breathing deeply for a while, the pain may go away. But sometimes it does not. Most runners just continue to run and walk with the side pain. In 50 years of running and helping others run, I've not seen any lasting negative effect from those who run with a side pain—it just hurts.

Tip: Some runners have found that side pain goes away if they tightly grasp a rock in the hand that is on the side of the pain. Squeeze it for 15 seconds or so. Keep squeezing 3-5 times as you breathe deeply.

You don't have to take in a maximum breath to perform this technique. Simply breathe a normal breath but send it to the lower lungs. You know that you have done this if your stomach goes up and down as you inhale and exhale. If your chest goes up and down, you are breathing shallowly.

Note: Never breathe in and out rapidly. This can lead to hyperventilation, dizziness and fainting.

I feel great one day... and not the next

If you can solve this problem, you could become a very wealthy person. There are a few common reasons for this, but there will always be "those days" when the body doesn't seem to work right, or the gravity seems heavier than normal—and you cannot find a reason. You should keep looking for the causes of this, in your journal. If you feel this way several times a week, for two or more weeks in a row, you may need more rest in your program.

1. Just do it. In most cases, this is a one-day occurrence. Most runners just put more walking into the mix, slow down, and get through it. Before doing a speed workout, however, make sure that there's not a medical reason for the "bad" feeling. I've had some of my best workouts after feeling very bad during the first few miles—or the first few speed repetitions.

2. Heat and/or humidity will make you feel worse. You will often feel better when the temperature is below 60F and miserable when 75F or above—and/or the humidity is high. If it is above 70F on a mile repeat day, do twice as many 800s instead, walking 3 minutes between each.

3. Low blood sugar can make any run a bad run. You may feel good at the start and suddenly feel like you have no energy. Every step seems to take a major effort.

4. Low motivation. Use the rehearsal techniques in the "mental toughness" chapter to get you out the door on a bad day. These have helped numerous runners turn their minds around—even in the middle of a run.

5. Infection can leave you feeling lethargic, achy, and unable to run at the same pace that was easy a few days earlier. Check the normal signs (fever, chills, swollen lymph glands, higher morning pulse rate, etc.) and at least call your doctor if you suspect something.

6. Medication and alcohol, even when taken the day before, can leave a hangover that doesn't affect any area of your life except for your running. Your doctor or pharmacist should be able to tell you about the effect of medication on strenuous exercise.

7. A slower start can make the difference between a good day and a bad day. When your body is on the edge of fatigue or other stress, it only takes a few seconds too fast per mile to push into discomfort or worse. A quick adjustment to a slightly slower pace before you get too tired can turn this around.

8. Caffeine can help because it gets the central nervous system working to top capacity. I feel better and my legs work so much better when I have had a cup of coffee an hour before the start of a run. Of course, those who have problems with caffeine should avoid it—or consult a doctor.

Cramps in the muscles

At some point, most people who run will experience an isolated cramp. These muscle contractions usually occur in the feet or the calf muscles and may come during a run or walk, or they may hit at random, afterward. Most commonly, they will occur at night, or when you are sitting around at your desk or watching TV in the afternoon or evening. When severe cramps occur during a run, you will have to stop or significantly slow down.

Cramps vary in severity. Most are mild but some can grab so hard that they shut down the muscles and hurt when they seize up. Massage, and a short and gentle movement of the muscle can help to bring most of the cramps around. Odds are that stretching will make the cramp worse, or tear the muscle fibers.

Most cramps are due to overuse—doing more than in the recent past, or continuing to put yourself at your limit, especially in warm weather. Look at the pace and distance of your runs and workouts in your training journal to see if you have been running too far, or too fast, or both.

- Continuous running increases cramping. Taking walk breaks more often can reduce or eliminate them. Several runners who used to cramp when they ran continuously, stopped cramping with a 10-30 second walk every 3-5 minutes during a long or fast run.

- During hot weather, a good electrolyte beverage (consumed after a run, or the day before a long runs) can help to replace the salts that your body loses in sweating. A drink like Accelerade, for example, can help in topping off these minerals when you drink approx. 6-8 oz every 1-2 hours, throughout the day, after a long run.

- On very long runs, however, the continuous sweating, especially when drinking a lot of fluid (more than 20 oz an hour), can push your sodium levels too low and produce muscle cramping. If this happens regularly, a buffered salt tablet has helped greatly—a product like Succeed. If you have any blood pressure or other sodium issues, check with your doctor first. Experts recommend drinking less than 20 oz (600 ml) an hour of fluid during a long run/marathon.

- Many medications, especially those designed to lower cholesterol, have muscle cramps as one of their known side effects. Runners who use medications and cramp should ask their doctor if there are alternatives.

Here are several ways of dealing with cramps:

1. Take a longer and more gentle warm-up.
2. Shorten your run segment—or take walk breaks more often.
3. Slow down your walk, and walk more.
4. Break your run up into two segments (not on long runs or speed workouts).
5. Look at any other exercise that could be causing the cramps.
6. Take a buffered salt tablet at the beginning of your exercise.
7. Form issues: Don't push off as hard, or bounce as high off the ground.
8. During speed workouts on hot days, walk more during the rest interval.

Note: If you have high blood pressure or similar problems, ask your doctor before taking any salt product.

Nausea or diarrhea

Sooner or later, virtually every runner has at least one episode with nausea or diarrhea. It comes from the buildup of total stress that you accumulate in your life—and specifically the stress of the workout. But stress is the result of many unique conditions within the individual. Your body produces the nausea/diarrhea (N/D) to get you to reduce the exercise, which will reduce the stress. Here are the common causes:

1. **Running too fast or too far** is the most common cause. Runners are confused about this, because the pace doesn't feel too fast in the beginning. Each person has a level of fatigue that triggers these conditions. Slowing down and taking more walk breaks will help you manage the problem. Speed training and racing will increase stress very quickly.

2. **Eating too much or too soon before the run.** Your system has to work hard when running, and it is also hard work to digest food. Doing both at the same time raises stress and results in nausea, etc. Having food in your stomach, in the process of being digested, is an extra stress and a likely target for elimination.

3. **Eating a high fat or high protein diet.** Even one meal that has over 50 % of the calories in fat or protein can lead to N/D hours later.

4. **Eating too much the afternoon or evening, the day before.** A big evening meal will still be in the gut the next morning, being digested. When you bounce up and down on a run, which you will, you add stress to the system, sometimes resulting in N/D.

5. **Heat and humidity** are major causes of these problems. Some people don't adapt well to even modest heat increases and experience N/D when racing (or doing speed sessions) at the same pace that did not produce the problem in cool weather. In hot conditions, everyone has a core body temperature increase that will result in significant stress to the system—often causing nausea, and sometimes diarrhea. By slowing down, taking more walk breaks, and pouring water over your head, you can manage this better.

6. **Drinking too much water *before* a run.** If you have too much water in your stomach, and you are bouncing around, you put stress on the digestive system. Reduce your intake to the bare minimum. Most runners don't need to drink any fluid before a run that is 60 minutes or less.

7. **Drinking too much of a sugar/electrolyte drink.** Water is the easiest substance for the body to process. The addition of sugar and/or electrolyte minerals, as in a sports drink, makes the substance harder to digest. During a run (especially on a hot day) it is best to drink only water if you have had N/D or other problems. Cold water is best.

8. **Drinking too much fluid (especially a sugar drink) too soon *after* a run.** Even if you are very thirsty, don't gulp down large quantities of any fluid during a short period of time. Try to drink no more than 6-8 oz, every 20 minutes or so. If you are particularly prone to N/D, just take 2-4 sips, every 5 minutes or so. When the body is very stressed and tired, it's not a good idea to consume a sugar drink (sports drink, etc). The extra stress of digesting the sugar can lead to problems.

9. **Don't let running be stressful to you.** Some runners get too obsessed about getting their run in or running at a specific pace. This adds stress to your life. Relax and let your run diffuse some of the other tensions in your life. When you are under a lot of "life stress" it's OK to delay a speed workout when the thought of fast running seems to increase your stress level. Take an easy jog!

Headache

There are several reasons why runners get headaches on runs. While uncommon, they happen to the average runner about 1-5 times a year. The extra stress that running puts on the body can trigger a headache on a tough day—even considering the relaxation that comes from the run. Many runners find that a dose of an over-the-counter headache medication takes care of the problem. As always, consult with your doctor about use of medication. Here are the causes/solutions.

Dehydration—if you run in the morning, make sure that you hydrate well the day before. Avoid alcohol the night before if you run in the mornings and have headaches. Also watch the salt in your dinner meal the night before. A good sports drink, taken throughout the day the day before, will help to keep your fluid levels and your electrolytes "topped off." If you run in the afternoon, follow the same advice leading up to your run, on the day of the run. If you are dehydrated an hour before a run, it doesn't help to drink a huge amount of water at that time—6-8 oz is fine.

Medications can often produce dehydration—There are some medications that make runners more prone to headaches. Check with your doctor.

Too hot for you—run at a cooler time of the day (usually in the morning before the sun gets above the horizon). When on a hot run, pour water over your head.

Being in the sun—Try to stay in the shade as much as possible. Wear a visor not a hat, making sure the band is not too tight.

Running a little too fast—start all runs more slowly, walk more during the first half of the run.

Low blood sugar level—be sure that you boost your BLS with a snack, about 30 minutes before you run. If you are used to having it, caffeine in a beverage can sometimes help this situation also—but caffeine causes headaches for a small percentage of runners.

If prone to migraines—generally avoid caffeine, and try your best to avoid dehydration. Talk to your doctor about other possibilities.

Watch your neck and lower back—If you have a slight forward lean as you run, you can put pressure on the spine—particularly in the neck and lower back. Read the form chapter in this book and see if running upright doesn't help the problem.

28 Staying Injury-Free

Note: For much more information in this area, see the new book PREVENTION AND CARE OF RUNNING INJURIES by Dr. David Hannaford and myself. It is available at www.JeffGalloway.com.

Because running and walking are activities that enabled our ancient ancestors to survive, we have the ability to adapt to these two patterns of motion if we use these principles:

- Walk or run at a gentle pace—and insert walk breaks from the beginning.
- Schedule sufficient rest between each workout.
- Exercise regularly—about every other day.
- When increasing exercise, do so very gradually, and reduce the intensity of the longer workout.
- The single greatest reason for improvement in running is not getting injured.

But inside each human is a personality trait that can compromise exercise enjoyment. I call this the "Type A overworker syndrome." Those who are candidates for Boston are prime candidates. When the workload is a bit too much, the body responds to the challenge at first. When the runner keeps pushing, without enough rest between, the body breaks at one of the "weak links." Here are some guidelines given as one exerciser to another.

Be sensitive to weak links
Each of us has a very few areas that take on more stress, and tend to register most of the aches, pains and injuries. The most common sites are the knees, the foot, the shins, and the hip. If you have a particular place on your knee that has been hurt before, and it hurts during or after exercise, take extra days off, and follow the suggestions concerning treating an injury, listed below.

How do you know that you are injured?
The following are the leading signs that you have an injury. If you feel any of the three below, you should stop your workout immediately and take some extra rest days (at least 2 days). Continuing to do the same exercise that irritated the tendon, muscle, etc., at the early stages of an injury, creates a dramatically worse injury—even during one workout. If you take 2-3 days off at the first symptom, you may avoid having to

stop exercise for 2-3 months by trying to push through the pain. It is always safer to err on the side of taking more time off when you first notice one of the following:

1. **Inflammation**—any type of swelling
2. **Loss of function**—the knee, foot, etc., doesn't work correctly
3. **Pain**—that does not go away when you walk for a few minutes

Losing conditioning

Studies have shown that you can maintain conditioning even when you don't run for 5 days. Surely you want to continue regular exercise if you can, but staying injury free has an even higher priority. So don't be afraid to take up to 5 days off when a "weak link" kicks in. In most cases you will only stop for 2-3 days.

Treatment

It is always best, at the first sign of a real injury, to see a doctor (or with muscle injury—a massage therapist) who wants to get you exercising again as soon as possible. The better doctors will explain what they believe is wrong (or tell you when he/she cannot come up with a diagnosis) and give you a treatment plan. This will give you great confidence in the process, which has been shown to speed the healing.

Treatments while you are waiting to see a doctor.

Unfortunately, most of the better doctors are so booked up that it may take several days and sometime weeks to see them. While waiting for your appointment, here are some things other exercisers have done when one of the weak links kick in:

- Take 2-5 days off from any activity that could irritate it.
- If the area is next to the skin (tendon, foot, etc.), rub a chunk of ice on the area(s)—constantly rubbing for 15 min until the area gets numb. Continue to do this for a week after you feel no symptoms. The chunk of ice must be rubbed constantly and directly on the tissue where the injury is located (ice bags and gel ice do virtually nothing).
- If the problem is inside a joint or muscle, call your doctor and ask if you can use prescription strength anti-inflammatory medication. Don't take any medication without a doctor's advice—and follow that advice.
- If you have a muscle injury, see a very successful sports massage therapist. Find one who has a lot of successful experience treating the area where you are injured. The magic fingers and hands can often work wonders.

- If cross training, such as water running, does not aggravate the problem, you can maintain conditioning by doing some, at least every other day.

Preventing injury

Having had over a hundred injuries myself, and then having worked with tens of thousands who have worked through aches and pains, I've developed the suggestions below. They are based upon my experience and are offered as one exerciser to another. I'm proud to report that since I started following the advice that I give others, I've not had an overuse injury in over 30 years.

Take 48 hours between strenuous workouts

Exercising longer or faster (for you) puts a lot more stress on the muscles, tendons, etc. Allowing tired muscles to rest for two days can work magic in recovery. Stair machine work should also be avoided during the 48-hour rest period (stair work uses the same muscles as running). Also avoid any other activities that seem to irritate the aggravated area.

Don't stretch!

I've come full circle on this. A high percentage of the exercisers who report to me, injured, have either become injured because they stretched or aggravated the injury by stretching. When they stop stretching, most have reported that the injury starts healing, in a relatively short period of time. The exception to this rule is in the treatment of Iliotibial band injury. For this injury alone, stretching the I-T band seems to help runners continue when the band tightens up.

Do the "toe squincher" exercise (prevention of foot and heel injuries)

This exercise can be done 10-30 times a day, on both feet (one at a time). Point the toes and squinch them until the foot cramps (only a few seconds). This strengthens the many little muscles in the foot that can provide a platform of support. It is particularly effective in preventing plantar fascia.

Don't increase total mileage or minutes more than 10% a week more than 2 weeks in a row.

Monitor your quantity of exercise with a log book or calendar. If you exceed the 10 per cent increase rule, take an extra day off.

Drop total mileage in half, every 3rd or 4th week—even when increasing by no more than 10 % per week.

Your logbook can guide you here also. You won't lose any conditioning and you'll help the body heal itself, and get stronger. A steady increase, week after week, does not allow the legs to catch up and rebuild.

Avoid a long stride—whether walking or running

Use more of a shuffle motion (feet close to the ground), and you'll reduce the chance of many injuries.

29 Injury Troubleshooting

Note: For more information see Prevention and Care of Running Injuries, by Hannaford and Jeff Galloway, available at www.JeffGalloway.com.

Quick Treatment Tips

For all injuries:

1. Take 3 days off from running or any activity that could aggravate the area.
2. Avoid any activity that could aggravate the injury.
3. As you return to running, stay below the threshold of further irritation with much more liberal walking.
4. Don't stretch unless you have iliotibial band injury. Stretching keeps most injuries from healing.

Muscle injuries:

1. Call your doctor's office and see if you can take prescription strength anti-inflammatory medication.
2. See a sports massage therapist who has worked successfully on many runners.

Tendon and foot injuries

1. Rub a chunk of ice directly on the area for 15 minutes every night (keep rubbing until the area gets numb—about 15 minutes).

Note: Ice bags, or gel ice don't seem to do any good at all.

2. Foot injuries sometimes are helped by a "boot" cast at first to let the problem start healing.

Knee injuries

1. Call your doctor's office to see if you can take prescription strength anti-inflammatory medication.
2. See if you can do a little gentle walking, sometimes this helps.
3. Sometimes the knee straps can relieve pain, ask your doctor.

4. Get a shoe check to see if you are in the right shoe (if you overpronate, a motion control shoe may help).
5. If you overpronate, an orthotic may help.
6. If you have internal knee pain, a glucosamine supplement may help.
7. If you have Iliotibial Band injury, using a foam roller has helped. Roll for 5 minutes before bed, and, if possible, 5 min each before and after a run.

Shin injuries

1. Rule out a stress fracture. In this case, the pain usually gets worse as you run—but check with your doctor. If it is a stress fracture, you must stop running for at least 8 weeks in most cases.
2. If the pain gradually goes away as you run on it, there is less worry of a stress fracture. This is probably a shin splint. If you stay below the threshold of irritating the shin muscle, you can run with shin splints as they gradually go away (check with doctor to be sure).
3. Take more walk breaks, run more slowly, etc.

Starting running before the injury has healed

With most running injuries, you can continue to run even while the injury is healing. But first, you must take some time off to get the healing started. If you do this at the beginning of an injury you will usually only need 2-5 days off. The longer you try to push through the problem, the more damage you produce and the longer it will take to heal. Stay in touch with the doctor at any stage of this healing/running process, follow his/her advice, and use your best judgment.

To allow for healing, once you have returned to running, stay below the threshold of further irritation. In other words, if the injury feels a little irritated when running at 2.5 miles, and starts hurting a little at 3 miles, you should run no more than 2 miles. And if your run-walk ratio is 5 min run/1 min walk, you should drop back to 2-1 or 1-1, or 30 seconds/30 seconds.

Take a day of rest between running days. With most injuries you can cross train to maintain conditioning, but make sure that your injury will allow this. Again, your doctor can advise.

Best cross training modes to maintain your running conditioning

Before doing any of these ask your doctor. Most are fine for most injuries. But some run a risk of irritating the injured area and delaying the healing process. For more information on this, see the chapter on cross training, in my Galloway's Book on Running, 2nd edition. Gradually build up the cross training, because you have to condition those muscles gradually also. Even walking is a great way to maintain conditioning if the injury and the doctor will allow it.

1. Running in the water—can improve your running form
2. Nordic Track machines
3. Walking
4. Rowing machines
5. Elliptical machines

There is much more information on specific injuries in my Galloway's Book on Running, 2nd edition. But here are some helpful items that I want to pass on as one runner to another.

30 Treatment Suggestions—From One Runner to Another

Note: For more information see Prevention and Care of Running Injuries, by Hannaford and Galloway, available at www.JeffGalloway.com

Knee pain

Most knee problems will go away if you take 5 days off. Ask your doctor if you can use anti-inflammatory medication. Try to figure out what caused the knee problem. Make sure that your running courses don't have a slant or canter. Look at the most worn pair of shoes you have, even walking shoes. If there is wear on the inside of the forefoot, you probably overpronate. If you have repeat issues with knee pain, you may need a foot support or orthotic. If there is pain under the kneecap, or arthritis, the glucosamine/chondroitin products have helped. The best I've found in this category is Joint Maintenance Product by Cooper Complete.

Outside of the Knee Pain—Iliotibial Band Syndrome

This band of fascia acts as a tendon, going down the outside of the leg from the hip to just below the knee. The pain is most commonly felt on the outside of the knee, but can be felt anywhere along the I-T band. I believe this to be a "wobble injury." When the running muscles get tired, they don't keep you on a straight running track. The I-T band tries to restrain the wobbling motion, but it cannot and gets overused. Most of the feedback I receive from runners and doctors is that once the healing has started (usually a few days off from running), most runners will heal as fast when you run on it as from a complete layoff. It is crucial to stay below the threshold of further irritation.

Treatment for Iliotibial Band Injury:

1. Self-massage using a foam roller. This device has helped thousands of runners get over I-T band. On my website **www.RunInjuryFree.com** is a picture of someone using a foam roller. Put the roller on the floor, lie on it using body weight to press and roll the area that is sore. It helps to warm up the area before a run, and to roll it out afterward. Especially helpful is to roll it 5 minutes before bed.

2. Massage Therapy: a good massage therapist can tell whether massage will help and where to massage. The two areas for possible attention are the connecting points of the connective tissue that is tight, and the fascia band itself, in several

places. "The stick" is a self massage roller device that has also helped many runners recover from I-T band as they run. As with the foam roller, it helps to warm up the area before a run, and to roll it out afterward.

3. Walking is usually fine—and usually you can find a run-walk ratio that works.

4. Direct ice massage on the area of pain: 15 minutes of continuous rubbing every night

5. Stretching: Stretch during a run if the I-T band tightens up. Here are several stretches that have worked for this injury.

Shin pain—"Shin Splints" or Stress Fracture

Almost always, pain in this area indicates a minor irritation called "shin splints" that allows running and walking as you heal. The greatest pain or irritation during injury is usually felt during the start of a run or walk, which gradually lessens or goes away as you run and walk. It takes a while to fully heal, so you must have patience, as you stay below the threshold of further irritation.

- Inside pain—posterior shin splints. Irritation of the inside of the leg, coming up from the ankle is called "posterior tibial shin splints" and is often due to overpronation of the foot (foot rolls in at push-off).

- Front of shin—anterior shin splints. When the pain is in the muscle on the front of the lower leg it is "anterior tibial shin splints." This is very often due to having too long a stride when running and especially when walking. Downhill terrain should be avoided as much as possible during the healing.

- Stress Fracture. If the pain is in a very specific place, and increases as you run, it could be a more serious problem: a stress fracture. This is unusual for beginning runners, but characteristic of those who do too much, too soon. It can also indicate low bone density. If you even suspect a stress fracture, do not run or do anything stressful on the leg and see a doctor. Stress fractures take weeks of no running, usually wearing a cast. They may also indicate a calcium deficiency.

Heel pain—Plantar Fascia

"The most effective treatment is putting your foot in a supportive shoe before your 1st step in the morning."

This very common injury (pain on the inside or center of the heel) is felt when you first walk on the foot in the morning. As you get warmed up, it gradually goes away, only to return the next morning. The most important treatment is to put your foot in a supportive shoe, before you step out of bed. Be sure to get a "shoe check" at a technical running store to make sure that you have the right shoe for your foot. If the pain is felt during the day, and is painful, you should consult with a podiatrist. Usually the doctor will construct a foot support that will surround your arch and heel. This does not always need to be a hard orthotic and is usually a softer one designed for your foot with build-ups in the right places.

The "toe squincher" exercise can help develop foot strength that will also support the foot. It takes several weeks for this to take effect. This is another injury that allows for running as you heal, but stay in touch with your doctor. The "squincher" is done by pointing your foot down, and contracting the muscles in the foot similar to making a hard "fist" with your hand.

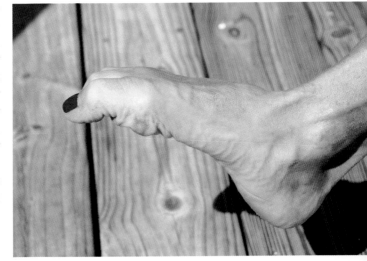

Back of the foot—Achilles tendon

The Achilles tendon is the narrow band of tendon rising up from the heel and connecting to the calf muscle. It is part of a very efficient mechanical system, acting like a strong rubber band to leverage a lot of work out of the foot, with a little effort from the calf muscle. It is usually injured due to excessive stretching, either through running or through stretching exercises. First, avoid any activity that stretches the tendon in any way. It helps to add a small heel lift to all shoes, which reduces the range of motion. Every night, rub a chunk of ice directly on the tendon. Keep rubbing for about 15 minutes, until the tendon gets numb. Bags of ice or frozen gels don't do any good at all in my opinion. Usually after 3-5 days off from running, the icing takes hold and gets the injury in a healing mode. Anti-inflammatory medication very rarely helps with the Achilles tendon, according to experts.

Hip and groin pain

There are a variety of elements that could be aggravated in the hip area. Since the hips are not prime movers in running, they are usually abused when you continue to push on, when very fatigued. The hips try to do the work of the leg muscles and are not designed for this. Ask your doctor about prescription strength anti-inflammatory medication, as this can often speed up recovery. Avoid stretching and any activity that aggravates the area.

Calf muscle

The calf is the most important muscle for running. It is often irritated by speedwork, and can be pushed into injury by stretching, running too fast when tired, by too many speed sessions without adequate rest between, and sprinting at the end of races or workouts. Bouncing too high and running a lot of hills can also trigger this injury.

Deep tissue massage has been the best treatment for most calf muscle problems according to my experience. Try to find a very experienced massage therapist who has helped lots of runners with calf problems. This can be painful but is about the only way to remove some bio-damage in the muscle. The "stick" can be very beneficial for working damage out of the calf muscle—on a daily basis (see our website for more information on this product).

Don't stretch! Stretching will tear the muscle fibers that are trying to heal. Avoid running hills, and take very frequent walk breaks as you return to running.

31 Products that Enhance Running

The Stick

This massage tool can help the muscles recover quicker. It will often speed up the recovery of muscle injuries or Iliotibial Band injuries (on the outside of the upper leg, between knee and hip). This type of device can help warm up the legs muscles and sore tendons (etc.) before running, and move some of the waste out afterward.

In working on the calf muscle (most important in running) start each stroke at the Achilles tendon and roll up the leg toward the knee. Gently roll back to the origin and continue, repeatedly. For the first 5 minutes your gentle rolling will bring additional blood flow to the area. As you gradually increase the pressure on the calf you will usually find some "knots" or sore places in the muscles. Concentrate on these as you roll over them again and again, breaking up the tightness. See **www. RunInjuryFree.com** for more info on this.

Foam Roller—self massage for I-T Band, Hip, etc.

The most popular size of this cylinder is approx. 6" in diameter and one foot long. This has been the most successful treatment device for Iliotibial band injury. In treating this injury, put the roller on the floor, and lie on you side so that the irritated I-T band area is on top of the roller. As your bodyweight presses down on the roller, roll up and down on the area of the leg you want to treat. Roll gently for 2-3 minutes and then let the body weight press down more.

This is a very effective pre-warm-up exercise for any area that needs more blood flow as you start. It is also very beneficial to use the roller after a run on the same areas. See **www.RunInjuryFree.com** for more info on this product.

Cryo-Cup—best tool for ice massage

Rubbing with a chunk of ice on a sore area (when near the skin) is very powerful therapy. I know of hundreds of cases of Achilles tendon problems that have been healed by this method. The Cryo-Cup is a very convenient device for ice massage. The plastic cup has a plastic ring that sits on top of it. Fill it up with water, then freeze. When you have an ache or pain, pour warm water over the cup to release it, giving you an ice "popsicle." Rub for about 15 minutes, constantly moving it on the area, until the tendon (or other area) is numb. When finished, fill up the cup again for use next time. It may surprise you, but rubbing with a plastic bag of ice—or a frozen gel product—does no good at all in most cases.

Endurox Excel

An hour before a long or hard workout, I take two of these Excel pills. Among the anti-oxidants is the active ingredient from ginseng: ciwega. Research has shown that recovery speeds up when this product is taken. I also use it when my legs have been more tired than usual for 2-3 days in a row.

Accelerade

This sports drink has a patented formula shown to improve recovery. It also helps to improve hydration. I recommend having some in the refrigerator as your fluid intake product taken throughout the day. Prime time to drink this regularly is the day before and after a long or strenuous workout day. During a prolonged speed training session, have a thermos nearby, for sipping on walk breaks.

Research has also shown that drinking Accelerade about 30 min before running can get the body's startup fuel (glycogen) activated more effectively, and may conserve the limited supply of this crucial fuel. For a discount on this product, go to www.JeffGalloway.com, and click on the "Accelerade" logo.

Endurox R4

This product has what I see as a "cult following" among runners. In fact, the research shows that the 4-1 ratio of carbohydrate to protein helps to reload the muscle glycogen more quickly. This means that the muscles feel bouncy and ready to do what you can do, sooner. There are other anti-oxidants that speed recovery. Prime time for this re-loading process is within 30 minutes of the finish of a run. For a discount on this product, go to www.JeffGalloway.com, and click on the "Accelerade" logo.

Jeff Galloway's Training Journal

Some type of journal is needed to organize, and track, your year-round plan. My own product can be ordered from www.JeffGalloway.com, autographed. It simplifies the process, with places to fill in information for each day.

Your journal allows you to organize your training in advance, which you can use as a daily workout guide. As you plan ahead and enter your data, you gain control over your training.

Other Galloway Books

For more information on these, visit www.JeffGalloway.com or www.phidippides.com

Other Galloway Books: training schedules, and gifts that keep on giving—even to yourself (Order them, autographed, from www.JeffGalloway.com)

Running – A Year Round Plan This is my most comprehensive training book. It weaves the training for several races at one time. You'll find daily workouts for 52 weeks, for three levels of runners: to finish, to maximize potential, and time improvement. It has the long runs, speed sessions, drills, hill sessions, all listed, in the order needed to do a 5K, 10K, Half and Marathon during one year. Resource material is included to help with many running issues.

Galloway Marathon FAQ There are over 100 of the most common questions I receive about marathon training and racing. You don't have to wade through pages of text to get the answers to your questions.

Running Until You're 100 In the chapter on joint health, you'll see in the research studies that runners have healthier joints than sedentary folks. In the chapter on the researched health benefits of exercise, an expert on longevity says that for every hour we exercise we can expect to get back 2 hours of life extension. Among the heroes section is an 85-year-old who recently finished his 700th marathon and will do 29 more this year. There are nutrition suggestions from Nancy Clark, training adjustments by decade, and many other helpful hints for running past the century mark.

Fit Kids—Smarter Kids This book is a handbook for parents, teachers and youth leaders in how to lead kids into fitness that is fun. A growing number of studies are listed that document how kids who exercise do better in academics, and in life. Nancy Clark gives tips on what to eat, and there's a chapter on childhood obesity—with the hope that others, like the author (a former fat kid) can turn things around. There are resources, successful programs, inspirational stories and much more.

Women's Complete Guide To Running & Women's Complete Guide to Walking By Barbara and Jeff Galloway. The section on woman-specific issues makes this book unique: pregnancy, menstrual issues, bra-fitting, incontinence, osteoporosis, inner organs shifting, menopause and more. There's a section for the unique problems of the "fabulously full figured" runners. Nutrition, fat-burning, motivation, starting up, aches and pains—all are covered in the book. There's also a section in each book written by famous sports nutritionist Nancy Clark.

Running and Fat Burning for Women By Barbara and Jeff Galloway. I've not seen another book that better describes the fat burning and accumulation process—with a strategy to take action. There are several important and inexpensive tools mentioned, with recipes, and specific suggestions about managing the calorie income and expenditure. There is also a section on women-specific issues.

Walking – the Complete Book Walkers now have a book that explains the many benefits, how to maximize them, with training programs for 5K, 10K, Half and Full Marathons. There is resource information on fat burning, nutrition, motivation and much more.

Running – Getting Started This is more than a state-of-the-art book for beginners. It gently takes walkers into running, with a 6-month schedule that has been very successful. Also included is information on fat-burning, nutrition, motivation, and body management. This is a great gift for your friends or relatives who can be "infected" positively by running.

Running Injuries Dave Hannaford is one of the best resources I've found in explaining why we get injured, and how to heal. He breaks down each major running injury to help you diagnose, treat and heal. I have written the section on prevention, based upon more than 30 years of no overuse injuries.

Galloway's Book On Running 2nd Edition This is the best seller among running books since 1984. Thoroughly revised and expanded in 2001, you'll find training programs for 5K, 10K, Half Marathon, with nutrition, fat burning, walk breaks, motivation, injuries, shoes and much more. This is a total resource book.

Galloway Training Programs This has the information you need to train for the classic event, the marathon. But it also has schedules for Half Marathon and 10 Mile. New in 2007, this has the latest on walk breaks, long runs, practical nutrition, mental marathon toughness and much more.

Half Marathon This new book provides highly successful and detailed training schedules for various time goals, for this important running goal. Information is provided on nutrition, mental preparation, fluids, race day logistics & check list, and much more.

Running – Testing Yourself Training programs for 1 mile, 2 mile, 5K, and 1.5 mile are detailed, along with information on racing-specific information in nutrition, mental toughness and running form. There are also some very accurate prediction tests that allow you to tell what is a realistic goal. This book has been used effectively by those who are stuck in a performance rut in 10K or longer events. By training and racing faster, you can improve running efficiency and your tolerance for waste products, like lactic acid.

Galloway's 5K/10K Running Whether you want to finish with a smile on your face, or have a challenging time goal in mind, this book is a total resource for these distances. There are schedules for a wide range of performances, how to eat, how to predict your performance, how long and how fast to run on long runs, drills to improve form and speed training. There is extensive information on mental preparation, breaking through barriers, practical nutrition and more.

Jeff Galloway's Training Journal

Some type of journal is recommended to organize, and track, your training plan. Jeff Galloway's Training Journal can be ordered from www.JeffGalloway.com, autographed. It simplifies the process, with places to fill in information for each day. There is also space for recording the unexpected thoughts and experiences that make so many runs come alive again as we read them.

*Running Schools and Retreats: Jeff conducts motivating running schools and retreats. These feature individualized information, form evaluation, comprehensively covering running, nutrition and fat burning.

*Nextfit—coaching through the iPod

As an extension of Jeff's training programs, he has teamed up with Podfitness.com to bring these workouts into your daily life. Now, you can have a custom program, during which Jeff coaches you through every training session on your iPod.

"My Podfitness training program is designed to reinforce what you've read here. Your program is designed expressly for you, and changes with you. You'll hear me throughout your workout, offering advice and encouragement. Plus, it lays your music in the background, which I think makes each run even more enjoyable." JG

Go to **www.Jeffgalloway.com** and click on the NexFit link.

Vitamins

I now believe that most runners need a good vitamin to help the immune system and resist infection. There is some evidence that getting the proper vitamin mix can speed recovery. The vitamin line I use is called Cooper Complete. Dr. Kenneth Cooper is behind this product. In the process of producing the best body of research on exercise and long-term health I've seen anywhere, he found that certain vitamins help in many ways.

Buffered Salt Tablets—to reduce cramping

If your muscles cramp on long or hard runs, this type of product may help greatly. The buffered sodium and potassium tablets get into the system more quickly. Be sure to ask your doctor if this product is OK for you (those with high blood pressure, especially). If you are taking a statin drug for cholesterol, and are cramping, it is doubtful that this will help. Ask your doctor about adjusting the medication before long runs.

Toys: Heart Monitors and GPS Devices

Heart Monitors

Left brain runners who are motivated by technical items and data tracking tell me that they are more motivated when using a heart monitor. Right brain runners who love the intuitive feel of running, find that the after-workout number crunching is often too intense, jolting them out of their transcendental state of running. But after talking with hundreds of both types of runners I realize that there are benefits—especially for runners who are doing speed training.

Once you determine your maximum heart rate, a good heart monitor can help you manage effort level. This will give you more control over the amount of effort you are spending in a workout, so that you can reduce overwork and recovery time. As they push into the exertion zone needed on a hard workout, left brain runners will gain a reasonably accurate reading on how much effort to spend or how much they need to back off to avoid a long recovery. Many "type A" runners have to be told to back off before they injure themselves. I've heard from countless numbers of these runners who feel that the monitors pay for themselves by telling them exactly how slow to run on easy days and how long to rest between speed repetitions during workouts. Right brain runners admit that they enjoy getting verification on the intuitive evaluation of effort levels. The bottom line is that monitors can tell you to go slow enough to recover, how long to rest during a speed session, and what your "red zone" is during a hard speed workout.

All devices have their "technical difficulties." Heart monitors can be influenced by local electronic transmissions and mechanical issues. Cell phone towers and even garage doors can interfere with a monitor on occasion. This is usually an incidental issue. But if you have an abnormal reading either high or low, it may be a technical abnormality.

Be sure to read the instruction manual thoroughly—particularly about how to attach the device to your body for the most accurate reading. If not attached securely you will miss some beats. This means that you are actually working a lot harder than you think you are.

I suggest that you keep monitoring how you feel, at each 5 % percentage increase toward max heart rate. Over time, you will get better at the intuitive feel, for example, of an 85 % effort when you should be at 80 %.

Get tested to determine max heart rate

If you are going to use a heart monitor, you should be tested to find your maximum heart rate. Some doctors (especially cardiologists) will do this. Other testing facilities include Human Performance Labs at Universities, and some health clubs and YMCA's. It is best to have someone supervising the test who is trained in cardiovascular issues. Sometimes the testing facility will misunderstand what you want. Be sure to say that you only need a "max heart rate test"—not a maximum oxygen uptake test. Once you have run for a couple of months with the monitor, you will have a clear idea what your max heart rate is from looking at your heart rate during a series of hard runs. Even on the hard speed workouts you can usually sense whether you could have worked yourself harder. But until you have more runs that push you to the limits, assume that your current top heart rate is within a beat or two of your current max that has been previously recorded.

Use the percentage of max heart rate as your standard

In general you don't want to get above 90 % of max heart rate during workouts. At the end of a long training program, this may happen at the end of a speed workout or two—and only for a short period. But your goal is to keep the percentage between 70 % and 80 % during the first half of the speed workout or longer run, and minimize the upward drift at the end of the workout.

Computing max heart rate percentage

For example, if your max heart rate is 200

90 % is 180
80 % is 160
70 % is 140
65 % is 130

On easy days, stay below 65 % of max heart rate

When in doubt, run slower. One of the major reasons for fatigue, aches and pains and burnout, is not running slowly enough on the recovery and fun days. Most commonly, the rate will increase at the end of a run. If this happens, slow down and take more walk breaks to keep it below 65 %.

Between speed repetitions, let the pulse rate drop below 65 % of max before doing another rep

To reduce the "lingering fatigue" that may continue for days after a hard workout, extend the rest interval walk until the heart rate goes down to this 65 % level or lower. At the end of the workout, if the heart rate does not drop below this level for 5 minutes, you should do your warm-down and call it a day—even if you have a few repetitions to go.

Run smoother on speed repetitions so that your heart rate stays below 80 % during speedwork

If you really work on running form improvements, you can minimize the heart rate increase by running more efficiently: keeping feet low to the ground, using a light touch, maintaining quick but efficient turnover of the feet. For more info on this, see the running form chapter in this book, or Galloway's Book on Running, Second Edition.

Morning pulse

If the chest strap doesn't interfere with your sleep, you can get a very accurate reading on your resting pulse in the morning. This will allow you to monitor over-training. Record the low figures each night. Once you establish a baseline, you should take an easy day when the rate rises 5 %-9 % above this. When it reaches 10 % or above, you should take an extra day off. Even if the heart rate increase is due to an infection, you should not run unless cleared by your doctor.

Use the "two minute rule" for the pace of long runs—not heart rate

Even when running at 65 % of max heart rate, many runners will be running a lot faster than they should at the beginning of long runs. Read the guidelines in this book for pacing the long runs, and don't be bashful about running slower.

But at the end of long runs, back off when heart rate exceeds 70 % of max

There will be some upward drift of heart rate, due to fatigue at the end of long runs. Keep slowing down if this happens, so that you stay around 70 % of max HR, or lower—even during the last few miles.

GPS and other distance-pace calculators

There are two types of devices for measuring distance, and both are usually very accurate: GPS and accelerometer technology. While some devices are more accurate than others, most will tell you almost exactly how far you have run. This provides the best pacing feedback I know of—except for running on a track—so that you don't start your runs too fast, etc.

Using the more accurate products gives you freedom. You can do your long runs without having to measure the course, or being forced to run on a repeated, but measured, loop. Instead of going to a track to do speed sessions, you can very quickly measure your segments on roads, trails or residential streets with GPS devices. If your goal race is on the track, I recommend that at least half of your speed sessions be run on the track. This relates to the principle of training called "specificity."

The GPS devices track your movements by the use of navigational satellites. In general, the more satellites, the more accurate the measurement. There are "shadows" or areas of buildings, forest or mountains in many areas where the signal cannot be acquired for (usually) short distances. You can see how accurate they are by running around a standard track. If you run in the middle of the first lane (not right next to the inside) you will be running about .25 mile.

The accelerometer products require a very easy calibration and have been shown to be very accurate. I've found it best on the calibration to use a variety of paces and a walk break or two in order to simulate what you will be doing when you run.

Some devices require batteries, and others can be re-charged. It helps to go to a technical running store for advice on these products. The staff there can often give you some "gossip" on the various brands and devices from the feedback they receive about how they perform in real life.

Photo & Illustration Credits:
Boston Marathon Photos: Victah Sailer, www.photorun.net
Photo p. 23: Barbara Galloway
Photos p. 24, 28, 162: Fay Foto, courtesy of the Boston Athletic Association
Cover photos: Victah Sailer, www.photorun.net; Fay Foto, courtesy of the Boston Athletic Association
Cover Design: Sabine Groten